Normandy

Normandy

A Father's Ship and a Son's Curiosity

David Cary

ISBN-13: 978-0692086919 (Carmichael Press)
ISBN-10: 0692086919
Library of Congress Control Number: 2017904649

Front illustration:
Ted Guzda and Bill Kesnick aboard the *PC 552* in front of one of the two aft 20 mm machine guns they manned on D-Day. Source: Bill Kesnick.

President Roosevelt: State of the Union Address, 07 Jan 1943. Source: National Archives and Records Administration (NARA).

Back illustration:
Soldier from the First US Infantry Division stares at the camera as injured comrades surround him near Omaha Beach. 06 June 1944. He has been identified as Nicholas Fina, who lived in Brooklyn, New York. Source: NARA.

Americans recover their dead from D-Day. Source: NARA.

I wish to have no Connection with any Ship that does not Sail fast for I intend to go in harm's way.

—Captain John Paul Jones, 16 November 1778

Dedication

This book is dedicated first and always to my wife, Stacy, who is the inspiration for everything good I do and who literally saved my life. If you have a spouse half as good, you are blessed beyond measure. Second, it is dedicated to my extended family, who have banded together in times of war and official government oppression. God has no use for those who are afraid to fight when called. Our parents got something right!

Lastly, this book is dedicated to my brothers and sisters who served in uniform in harm's way. Make our efforts be for a purpose. Please keep the promises that were made to us.

Please honor the gallant USS PC 552 and its officers and crew by providing a review of their story on Amazon at:
https://www.amazon.com/Normandy-Fathers-Ship-Sons-Curiosity/dp/0692086919
Click on "Reviews" and add yours.

Table 1. Ship history

Figure 1. The USS *PC 552* flying all flags

The flags read "Nan, Baker, Uncle, Yoke" (see Figure 2 below), *PC 552*'s signal. A modern translation is "November, Bravo, Uniform, Yankee." Source: Sara Pilling, daughter of Lt. J. Ross Pilling.

Builder	Sullivan Dry Dock and Repair Co. of Brooklyn, NY
Ordered	01 April 1941
Laid	20 May 1941
Launched	13 February 1942
Commissioned	29 July 1942
Decommissioned	18 April 1946
Declared surplus	24 April 1946
Struck	05 June 1946
Sold	06 Dec 1946 to the Maritime Commission, predecessor to MARAD (maritime administration)
Action	Battle of the Atlantic Battle of Normandy

Figure 2. Reproductions of the signal flags identifying the USS *PC 552*

Figure 3. Commissioning photograph of the crew of the USS *PC 552*

Based on deck log entries, I believe this image was taken on or shortly after 10 August 1942. Source: official US Navy photograph.

The officer on the far right is Lt. William Carr. The officer to Carr's left is Lt. Theodore Fuller, whom the crew called "the little admiral" for his strictness. The officer in the center is the commanding officer, Lt. Donald McVickar. This date would make the officer on the far left Lt. Karnig Mooshian, the executive officer.[1]

The man at the top on the far left is Thomas Williams, the cook; the darker man is Arsenio Lupisan, originally from the Philippines; and the man behind and to the left of Lt. Fuller is Bill Kesnick. Roland Stine was identified as the man to the left of and behind Arsenio Lupisan.

---

[1] Per telephone conversation with Bill Kesnick on 15 September 2017.

Contents

Illustrations

·   ·   ·   ·   ·   ·   ·   ·   ·

TABLES

Foreword

I first met author Dave Cary and his wife, Stacy, while they were political activists working against unwarranted governmental interference with Texas families. I was serving as a Texas state senator at the time and could not help but notice their zeal as they crisscrossed the capitol promoting family freedom.

As servants of the public, we see all sorts of people with varying views. Upon closer observance, I realized the Carys had successful professional backgrounds, and I found their views well reasoned. Between them, Stacy and Dave have earned military experience, worked as oil wildcatters, been part of a NASDAQ-listed technology start-up, and developed real estate, and now Dave has written this fascinating book.

And a timely book it is. For America, World War II started when Pearl Harbor was attacked more than seventy-five years ago. The men and women who responded in that horrible time of need, our fathers and mothers, are fading away fast. Their stories need to be told. Readers will enjoy this captivating tale of how ordinary men—strangers together in a small, ordinary ship—found themselves at the Battle of Normandy.

John Carona

Former Texas state senator
Chairman and chief executive officer, Associa
Dallas, Texas

Preface

I always knew my father-in-law, Nick Stine, was at the Battle of Normandy. Like many who have gone through such experiences, he did not talk about it much until he was in his later years. I always felt he believed that of all the people close to him, I was the one who could relate best to his experiences, because of our shared military background. One day, he requested I find out what happened to his ship. Thanks to the magic of the Internet, I was able to make some quick initial discoveries. The more I discovered, the more I wanted to know. This became a self-perpetuating cycle, and the result is this book about the *PC 552*.

**Figure 4.
Vietnam-era
"steel pot"**
An excellent
pillow under
certain
conditions.

My military experience was as a Vietnam-era infantry sergeant. I spent most of my time patrolling the jungles of Central America. Initially, trying to relate to the US Navy of World War II was as alien to me as trying to relate to a denizen of the far side of the moon. The "tin can" *Nick* bounced around in was a naval warship; the "tin can" *I* bounced around in was my steel helmet. In the navy world, enlisted men focused on their occupation specialty, and he mastered his as a radioman, one of a few aboard; in my world, everyone was a rifleman. We all focused on the M-16 and other small arms and tactics. He learned the workings of his ship; I learned how to move through the jungle quickly and plan our patrols from water source to water source. He came home to a grateful nation, while I learned to keep quiet about my military past to prevent retribution.

These were different times with different goals, philosophies, and languages—not only between the two services but between the two eras. Stop and think about it: The time that separates us from them is about the same time that separates them from the American Civil War (as of 2018). And yet my mother knew people who fought in the American Civil War—just as you may know people who fought in World War II.

The men of that generation are mostly gone now. My father was one of them. The name of John Robert Cary is inscribed in the courthouse of Boulder, Colorado, as a son who marched to war in the nation's time of need. My father-in-law is another. Nick Stine was one of the last living former crew members of his ship, the USS *PC 552*. This book captures the story of those times before it is lost forever.

Acknowledgments

There are so many people to acknowledge that it makes almost no sense to acknowledge *anyone* and risk forgetting others. Accordingly, I acknowledge my wife, who constantly had to listen to me talking about "that ship." Thank you for bringing me home. I love you.

Julia Cary, Roland "Nick" Stine's granddaughter and my daughter, designed and created this book's cover. Julia, you are the smile in my heart.

Lastly, I acknowledge my editor, Kellie Osborne, who added so much value to this book. I now know why authors always acknowledge their editors.

Prologue

This is the story of a minor ship that wound up at the Battle of Normandy during World War II. Yes, it was a US Navy warship, but it was of one of the smallest classes; in fact, the US government built only 315 of its type. This is also the story of that ship's crew—mostly ordinary men from all walks of life and from all over the United States who were called to duty, did what they had to do, and went home to success or failure. Many of these men were outwardly brave but inwardly frightened,

Figure 5. "Dare You to Say or Think You Do Not Feel"
Publisher: General Cable Corporation. C. C. Beall, 1943.
Source: NARA, 514103.

unwilling to let anyone know they were scared. Neither the ship nor its crew was the type stories are told about. There was no glamour here—and yet they have a story.

The US Navy built and crewed *PC 552* in haste at the beginning of the dark days of the Battle of the Atlantic. It took on the rightfully feared German U-boats; escorted invasion craft to the United Kingdom; and finally participated in the D-Day invasion of Normandy as a control vessel, one of the ships closest to shore, at the Fox Green sector of Omaha Beach. The *PC 552* came under attack from small-arms fire, aircraft, and the hated German 88 artillery; it returned blow for blow. It continued to battle German warcraft until the Germans surrendered in May 1945, then recrossed the Atlantic for an overhaul prior to being sent to finish the job with the Japanese in the Pacific. The atom bomb intervened in the meantime. In the end, the ship was ignobly scrapped as quickly as it had been built—the war was over, and the navy considered *PC 552* surplus.

This is also part of the story of a mighty nation of civilians, merely gifted amateurs when it came to this war business, who rose with an energy and dynamism that only a truly free and committed society could have achieved. When the United States declared war, many men drilled with broomsticks, as there were not enough bolt-action Springfield rifles to go around.

Seemingly overnight, the nation mobilized from having an army smaller than Portugal's to building one of the mightiest seen on the face of the earth. The nation's military might peaked at 12.4 million men and women in uniform, well armed with the semiautomatic M-1 rifle, the envy of most of the combatants; the B-29 bomber; and the atom bomb.

The *PC 552* was a part of that story. The military made many mistakes in the rapid mobilization: sailors were assigned to the ship, then reassigned shortly thereafter to another ship; ship design was changed on the fly; and when launched, the ship initially bumbled the war effort. But the ship and its crew quickly learned the craft of war…and learned it well. They served in the defining times of the twentieth century: World War II and the culminating event of D-Day.

As impressive as the mobilization was, there is an even more impressive story concerning the rapid *de*mobilization, which was performed with the same energy and efficiency as was the mobilization. Both were performed with amazing directness and sense of purpose.

This all occurred against the backdrop of what was going on in the wider world the *PC 552* faced. Many events occurred in rapid succession on the world's stage, and those frightening episodes were on every American's lips. Most are largely forgotten these days, except by a few people now in their nineties who have run their race and are waiting to be called home. People forget how scary those times were.

1
The Happy Times

American society often forgets that the United States badly lost the opening stages of the Battle of the Atlantic. The nation was woefully unprepared for the Germans' unrestricted submarine warfare. Merchant vessels plied up and down the Atlantic coast and to South America without escorts. American cities were not blacked out, and U-boat commanders often could sight their prey easily, as massive dark shadows highlighted against the bright coastal-city lights.

To add to this pressure, the United States' initial job was to safeguard the shipment of war materials, the primary of which was fuel from the States and South America, as it traveled from the Americas across the Atlantic. This was often collected at

> **Military Date Format**
> This book uses a modified version of the US military date format (e.g., 25 May 2000). This is the same format the men of the *PC 552* used.

Guantanamo Bay, Cuba, and consolidated at New York prior to being shipped to the United Kingdom and the Soviet Union. Because of how the shipping lanes were deployed, this made a major naval battle area of the North Atlantic coast, the Gulf, the Caribbean, the northwestern coastal areas of South America, and later the Atlantic itself.

The Venezuelan oil fields were a major source of oil. The largest oil refinery in the world was on Curacao (held by the Dutch), and the largest refinery in the British Empire was on Trinidad. There was another major refinery at Aruba (also held by the Dutch) in the Caribbean. Major shipping came down the Mighty Mississippi to New Orleans, where it was consolidated and forwarded on through the Gulf of Mexico to the Allies. Lastly, the Guianas in South America were the major source for aluminum ore, which was critical for aircraft manufacturing.

The United States was unprepared for this warfare and was slow to adopt effective countermeasures. Cities stayed lit; lighthouses continued to operate, which helped the enemy navigate; and ships ran during the night with navigation lights blazing. The States had already "lent" fifty destroyers to the United Kingdom and was short of the naval resources needed to address the problem at home. Only a few obsolete destroyers, some yachts converted to antisubmarine service (precursor patrol crafts), and a few coast-guard cutters were available.[2]

When the British and Americans first faced submarine warfare in World War I, there were two schools of thought: (1) send ships individually with the hope they would not be noticed or (2) send well-defended convoys sure to be detected but able to protect themselves. It was soon clear the convoy system was superior, as it ensured the most ships got through, and this knowledge carried forward to World War II. The American naval authorities initially refused to convoy shipping. Most of

Figure 6. The sinking of the *Dixie Arrow*
26 March 1942. Source: Outer Banks History Center.

---

[2] Brian John Murphy, "Sharks in American Waters," *America in WWII*, October 2006.

America's antisubmarine-capable craft were sent on an individual basis to hunt U-boats in the major shipping lanes. Unfortunately, U-boats were attracted to shipping, not antisubmarine vessels. The antisubmarine vessels found nothing, because they were avoided by the submarines, which continued to attack shipping, largely without cost.

Some historians blamed Admiral Ernest King, the director of the US Navy's operations, planning, and administration for the initial decision not to convoy. The truth is, when one has only a few less than ideal vessels—as the navy did—convoying is not practical. The munitions had to be shipped, so he decided to go ahead without convoying and accept the risk, but he also began a crash program to build more antisubmarine capability.

So many ships were sunk off Cape Hatteras, North Carolina, that the area earned the nickname "Torpedo Junction." The residents got used to hearing distant explosions at almost any time of day or night; the houses shook, and the walls cracked. They had no choice but to get used to it. This culminated in the sinking of the oil tanker the *Dixie Arrow*.[3]

Water is a better conductor of sound than air, so as these ships sank, people listening on sonar could hear the shrieking metal and ultimate slam as

Figure 7. Somebody blabbed
US government work for hire.
Source: public domain.

---

[3] Kevin P. Duffus, "When World War II Was Fought Off North Carolina's Beaches," *Tar Heel Junior Historian*, Spring 2008.

the water pressure collapsed the bulkheads. That was the sound of men being simultaneously crushed and drowned. Sometimes sailors on other ships could hear their screams.

Flaming hulks often illuminated the night skies along the Atlantic and Gulf coasts, and wreckage and bodies washed ashore in the mornings. Beachgoers in Jacksonville, Florida, on 10 April 1942 watched a U-boat rise in broad daylight and use its deck guns to attack and sink the ship *Gulf of America* with no consequences. On 15 June of that year, two American ships were torpedoed in broad daylight. Swimmers at Virginia Beach, Virginia, witnessed ships burning and men dying in the waters.

Enemies sank so much shipping in those days that American authorities were afraid to let the public know. The "loose lips sink ships" campaign started at this time, and some believe it began in part to keep the public from learning of those significant losses.

The Germans referred to this period as the "Second Happy Time" (the "First Happy Time" being when they initially went after the British). They could not believe their good fortune: they were able to inflict enormous damage at little cost to themselves.

By July 1942, U-boat commanders began to report back that the Americans were starting to convoy and were doing so with adequate escorts. The Americans had begun a crash-course project of building antisubmarine capability, including ships and planes, as Franklin D. Roosevelt's "Arsenal of Democracy" began to ramp up. As the danger to the U-boats increased, the Germans withdrew, and the battle moved to the east.

This initial phase for the Battle of the Atlantic was finally over in (roughly) August 1942. By the end, Germany had sunk more than six hundred ships off the East Coast and in the Gulf of Mexico, killed more than five thousand sailors, and destroyed 22 percent of America's tanker fleet. It was a major strategic win for the Axis powers.

The navy focused on producing patrol craft (PC), as they could be built much more quickly than could traditional destroyer escorts. These are the times the *PC 552* was born into and the purpose for which it was born.[4] Like man, the *PC 552* was "born unto trouble as the sparks fly upward" (Job 5:7, KJV).

---

[4] Brian John Murphy, "Sharks in American Waters," *America in WWII*, October 2006.

2

Patrol Craft (PC)

We don't speak about patrol craft because they are not huge like aircraft carriers or battleships. It's impossible to understand the *PC 552* and its crew and times without understanding what a patrol craft is. In the dispatches of the time, they were often mistakenly referred to as "torpedo boats," even though they had crews ten

Table 2. Specifications (*General Information Book*)[5]	
Displacement	280 tons (lt), 450 tons (fl)
Length	173 feet 8 inches
Beam	23 feet 1 inch
Draft	10 feet 10 inches
Installed power	Two diesel engines Type 16-V-9 ½ X 12R. 16 cylinders. General Motors Corporation.
Speed	20.2 knots (23.2 mph)

times as large and did not fire torpedoes. Because of their small size, speed, and maneuverability, patrol craft were the workhorses of transoceanic convoys and amphibious assaults. Many patrol craft sailors felt their efforts were unrecognized.

When one speaks with former crew members and their descendants, one senses the loving pride they felt and still feel. The commanding officer on D-Day, Lt. Frank Pierce, spent his later years building a beautiful model of the *PC 552*. Lt. J. Ross Pilling, another

---

[5] *General Information Book for PCs 552–555*. Issued by the US Navy. Cover page missing (basically the ships' owner's manual). Source: National Archives and Records Administration (NARA), College Park, MD.

commander, kept more mementoes of the *PC 552* than he did of other, supposedly more important, ships he served on.

Description

Patrol craft were 173 feet long and were originally built for antisubmarine warfare (ASW), convoy-escort duty, and coastal patrols.[6] The US Navy defined a ship as a vessel 200 feet or more in length; anything else was deemed a craft. In the European theater, patrol craft served as transatlantic convoy defense during the Battle of the Atlantic (1941–1943) until enough destroyer escorts (DE) had been built to take over.[7] Subsequently, PCs were used to patrol the coasts of Europe and the Pacific and to guide and control amphibious landings. From 07 December 1941 to 01 October 1945, a total of 315 steel PCs (including *PC 552*) and 444 wooden PCs were built. The military formally designated wooden PCs as submarine chasers (SCs) on 08 April 1943 to clear up confusion.[8] Patrol craft

Figure 8. The Fighting Donald Duck
This is a photo of the actual *Fighting Donald Duck* painted on the side of the *PC 552*. Source: Sara Pilling, daughter of one of the *PC 552*'s commanders, Lt. J. Ross Pilling.

---

[6] Mark Matyas, "173-Foot Steel-Hull Patrol Craft," Patrol Craft Sailor Association.

[7] Kesnick Guzda, "The Stamford Historical Society Presents," The Stamford Historical Society. http://www.stamfordhistory.org/ww2_kesnickguzda.htm.

[8] Greg H. Williams, *World War II US Navy Vessels in Private Hands* (Jefferson, NC: McFarland & Company Inc., 2013), 199.

were among the smallest US naval vessels in existence that could officially cross the Atlantic on their own power.

The Donald Duck Navy

Most sailors referred to the PCs as the "Donald Duck Navy," although where that name came from, no one knows. An early use of the symbol of Donald Duck on a PC was by Jim Dickie, a signalman on *PC 564*. Dickie painted the *Fighting Donald Duck* on the starboard wing of the bridge. From there, it seems to have been spread as a badge of honor. The Fighting Donald Duck—with his binoculars on the lookout for enemy submarines, his ash cans to the rear, and his depth charges mounted on a K-gun and ready to throw at a moment's notice—became the unofficial symbol of the Donald Duck Navy. It even made it to the letterhead of the Submarine Chaser Training Center in Miami, Florida.[9] The Fighting Donald Duck symbol was a source of pride.

Class

PC 552 was a Class 461 ship. Class 461 patrol craft were built for the US Navy from 1941 to 1944. They were called Class 461 because the first one built, which began the series, was *PC 461*. The first of the class to enter service was the *PC 470*.[10] The Class 461 was designed to be produced rapidly and in large numbers, to be an effective antisubmarine vessel, and to relieve larger vessels from convoy duty.

Living conditions

Go to your driveway or a parking lot and pace off a length 173 feet

---

[9] Wm. J. Veigele, *PC Patrol Craft of World War II* (Santa Barbara, CA: Astral Publishing, 1998), 400.

[10] Some sources say the first Class 461 PC deployed was *PC 471*, but they are wrong. The *PC 470* started life as a Q ship, a decoy for U-boats.

long. (A typical adult's pace is a bit less than a yard long, so this distance would be about sixty paces.) Now pace off twelve feet (four paces) perpendicularly from each side of the line a little bit advanced from the middle of the first line. Picture in your mind a sharp oval shape from those two dimensions, more sharply tapered to the rear than the front, and sit down in the middle of it. That is a small area—and it's about the size of an average patrol craft. In fact, one crew member stated that pulling alongside a typical American warship in the *PC 552* felt like paddling a canoe.

Now imagine this shape crammed with weapons, sonar, radar, machinery for operations, and two massive engines. Moreover, imagine about sixty (often more) men crammed in and around that weaponry and equipment and living, working, sweating, and fighting; sheltering from fierce north Atlantic gales; and feverishly pursuing U-boats that could turn and destroy them if given a break. There was nowhere crew members could be on that ship without constantly bumping into and jostling one another. Imagine the close quarters; opportunities for frayed nerves; and most of all,

Figure 9. False stockings
President Roosevelt issued Executive Order 9024 to establish the War Production Board (WPB) to ensure critical materials were used for the war effort. Limitations Order L-85 prohibited unnecessary uses of material such as frills and bows and upturned cuffs and regulated the maximum length of hemlines. Some women, in a burst of patriotism, raised their hemlines even higher to save material for "the boys."
Nylon stockings were in particularly short supply, and women resorted to simulating them with paint. Source: Pinterest.

the smells. During bad weather, most sailors stayed below decks.

During World War I, German sailors referred to their submarines as pig boats. That is because they had no patrol craft to compare them to. Patrol craft were basically massive weapons and engines surrounded by enough ship to keep them afloat. They didn't have much fresh water to begin with, and what they needed was supposed to come from the solar-powered distillers. These rarely worked because of the ship's violent pitching, and the ship itself needed fresh water for its operation.[11] This meant there was none to spare for niceties such as personal hygiene. Sailors were allowed to wash their hands and teeth twice a day with fresh water; they did everything else with salt water. Salt water causes itching, so crew members did *not* embrace this. Washing clothes was difficult, and as a practical matter, many crew members just slept in their clothes and longed for port.

> "However, PCs have a pitch all of their own and that is what does it. We climb a wave, stay there and vibrate a little, and then, Boom! At first I was afraid the ship would capsize and we'd all be lost. After a while, I was so sick I was afraid maybe we'd live through it. We lived through it, all right, and in several more trips we got over our seasickness."
> Grundman, Vernon H., "It's Rugged," *Our Navy*, 01 May 1945.

Patrol craft were famous for being rough sailors. Story after story attested to the roughness of a patrol craft's ride. When building a ship, there is a trade-off between the stability of the ride and seaworthiness, and the standard patrol craft was a very *seaworthy* vessel. On paper, they were designed to withstand a roll to each side of 110°. No, this is not a typo: they could roll 20° past a vertical deck.[12] Rolls of 60° to each side were common. Many reported seeing

---

[11] Wm. J. Veigele, *PC Patrol Craft of World War II* (Santa Barbara, CA: Astral Publishing, 1998).

[12] Ibid., 59.

such corkscrew rolls, with a third of the deck awash with the seas; onlookers would watch the ship shake itself off like a wet terrier and right itself, only to plunge the other side of the deck underwater, time after time. Sources report the gun crews on the main deck often found themselves standing in water up to their shoulders, first to the right, then to the left. It was a young man's game. The constantly awash decks also caused continuous electrical shorts. Sometimes these shorts would make the radar and mousetraps (antisubmarine weapon—see "Armament") not function. It turns out electronics do not like to be constantly drenched with salt water.

Figure 10. Kilroy was here
Nothing was more iconic of the World War II American military than the Kilroy graffiti. It was found all over the world, and soldiers swore that when they took an enemy position, they would find this graffiti was already there.
Source: Pinterest

Eating tables had a fiddle dam, a raised border around the table to catch plates before they slid off, although many crew members held their plates in their laps. Some days, because of their chronic seasickness, the crew ate mostly soda crackers.

Remember that time when you first experimented with alcohol? You overindulged and wound up worshipping at the porcelain altar all night. Over the next few days, as you slowly took back the attributes of a human, you swore you would never touch the stuff again. Seasickness is much worse than that, and for some sailors, it was chronic—day after day after day. Imagine the aroma enhancement

18

generated by filled puke buckets everywhere. Some really sick sailors took refuge in the lifeboats, which were covered with a tarp and were relatively dark and quiet.

We can add to this the constant slamming into the thin-skinned hulls of the ships from the explosions of depth charges. Look at your little finger from the side. It is a bit more than five-sixteenths of an inch thick[13]—thicker than the steel plates that made up the ship's hull. Imagine sleeping with the machinists near the waterline. The sound of the rushing water inches from one's face was peaceful but frightening during a howling storm with waves constantly pounding into the side. When a six-hundred-pound depth charge went off, it slammed into the ship, jarring everyone aboard. The

Figure 11. World War II service flag
Families showed these banners in their windows. A gold star was awarded for each family member who died in the war, and a blue star was for each living family member in uniform.
Source: Library of Congress.

shocks slammed into the ankles, knees, and backs of the men standing on deck over and over again. Men learned to flex their knees

---

[13] Many sources say the hull plates were three-sixteenths of an inch thick, but some sources say they were three-eighths of an inch. After almost a century, it is not clear which measurement is correct, so I have chosen the most likely thickness. In truth, the shipbuilders probably used whatever they had at hand.

to absorb the shock and to not rest their weary heads on a bulkhead—if a depth charge or a mine went off, the concussion from the explosion translated directly through the bulkhead into their heads, scrambling their brains. These five-sixteenth-inch plates were welded onto a frame made of the keel, ribs, and crossmembers, and many photos corroborate that, over time spent battling howling winds and throwing depth charges, the plates visibly sank into the frame. The sleek, new ships launched with such fanfare soon began to look haggard. Perhaps the men did, also.

Names

The US Navy usually did not provide traditional names to patrol craft; instead, their names were their designations. As the documents of the time show, the name of *this* ship was the USS *PC 552*.[14] Many sailors expressed resentment that their beloved ships were considered unworthy of a real name. Belatedly, in the 1950s, the navy assigned names to those few patrol craft that still existed. They were assigned the names of secondary US cities, cities with populations of between five hundred thousand and three million people. Former shipmates were often puzzled by the names assigned.

Armament[15]

To further understand these men and their times, we need to understand the weapons they fought with. Everyone in a combat role knows it is important that all weapons perform well at all times; accordingly, they are lovingly cared for. It is not uncommon for a veteran to recall every nick and bur in an oiled, gleaming weapon

---

[14] Wm. J. Veigele, *PC Patrol Craft of World War II* (Santa Barbara, CA: Astral Publishing, 1998), 36.

[15] Ibid.

forty years later while nodding over his thoughts as his grandchildren play on his knee.

Description

Patrol craft were designed primarily for antisubmarine warfare and minesweeping, and the armament reflected this. A secondary group of arms were antisurface and antiaircraft. As ASW ships, PCs were equipped with both sonar and radar to detect enemy submarines, although these were added later. Once U-boats were detected, the PCs brought their weapons to bear.

Antisubmarine weapons

There were three major types of ASWs, each designed for a particular purpose. I describe them here, then explain the mystery we encountered trying to understand what weapons the *PC 552* had.

Figure 12. The *PC 552* fires a depth charge
Date unknown but probably 1942 or 1943. Source: Sara Pilling.

Everyone who has watched a World War II navy movie has seen those drums filled with six hundred pounds of explosives. As the drums drift down, bubbles trickle up, and suddenly, there is a massive explosion, which we know happened because we see the camera shake. These depth charges, colloquially referred to as "ash cans," were rolled off the ship's stern on two release racks and set to explode at a predefined depth, usually three hundred feet—maximum periscope depth. They were set at this depth because no one really knew what depth a submarine was at in the early days. Ash cans had to explode within fifteen feet of the submarine to destroy it, but they were quite respected nonetheless. No U-boat ever sought the honor of gratuitously receiving a depth-charge barrage. A major drawback was that U-boats were detected through sonar—this is to say, through listening. Once an ash can barrage went off, the echoes and reverberations made further detection very difficult.

The ship could also throw depth charges to each side using "K guns," the name of which was inspired by their shape. Between two to four were mounted, equally divided on each side of the ship. An explosive charge lifted the teardrop-shaped depth charge, which held three hundred pounds of explosives, up and to the sides of the ship. Between the ash cans and the K guns, a patrol craft could throw out a pattern of eight to ten depth charges over a wide area. In both instances, the ship had to be moving, or the depth charges could destroy the ship. Of course, these K gun depth charges also sabotaged the acoustics, which made for loss of contact.

Figure 13. Mousetrap
Four missile launcher "antisubmarine projector Mark 20s," known colloquially as a "mousetrap." Source: NARA.

The last type is the mousetrap, which was introduced later in the war. Mousetraps were two launching racks, each with four ahead-thrown sixty-pound rocket-propelled charges that fell in an elliptical pattern and armed as they dropped through the water. At three hundred yards, the ellipse was eighty yards wide. There were eight bombs in total, and each bomb was loaded with thirty-three pounds of TNT. The racks were flush with the deck until used. In action, they were elevated and loaded with the bombs for firing. Because the racks were fixed, they were aimed with the ship's direction and fired when the ship was on an even keel. Most importantly, a rocket exploded only when it made contact with a target, which caused the others in proximity to explode also. This had the added benefit of not destroying the acoustics unless the rocket made actual physical contact with a U-boat. Larger vessels had hedgehogs, which could be aimed independently of the ship's position. Both hedgehogs and mousetraps were a major improvement over ash cans and K guns.

Figure 14. Three-inch/50-caliber gun of *PC 552*
Date unknown but probably 1944.
Source: Heber Pierce, son of Lt. Frank Pierce, the commanding officer on D-Day.

With all this, a patrol craft could throw antisubmarine explosives to the front, to the rear, and to each side. In all instances, if a ship dropped a depth charge in shallow water, the explosion could damage the ship itself—a greater danger in the Caribbean, where the water was often shallow.

Figure 15. Bofors 40 mm/56-caliber ship machine gun
Source: NARA.

Surface-to-surface weapons

When the *PC 552* was commissioned, it had two three-inch/50-caliber guns, known as the Main Battery. They were pedestal mounted and had trainer and pointer seats. It took a trigger and a foot pedal to fire them. This was a more formidable weapon than it sounds: the gun fired a projectile three inches in diameter, and the barrel was 50 calibers long (150 inches). Its purpose

Figure 16. 20 mm Oerlikon
Source: NARA.

was for surface warfare. The three-inch/50-caliber gun could also serve as an antiaircraft weapon. As mean as the gun looks, however, it was not a match for the German or Japanese submarines, both of which had superior armament.

Antiaircraft weapons

When commissioned, the *PC 552* had two 20 mm Oerlikons mounted on the chart house (*PCs 553, 554,* and *555* each had one more mounted on the chart house); these were known as the Secondary Battery. The Oerlikon was a manually operated air-cooled weapon mounted on a pedestal. The gunner was shoulder strapped to it. One or two loaders fed loaded magazines to the gun and exchanged hot barrels. If the barrels were not exchanged, they melted. The Oerlikon was capable of firing 450 rounds per minute and had a maximum range of four thousand yards. It replaced 50-caliber machine guns, which the navy determined to be too slow to take on enemy aircraft.

Some patrol craft had Bofors 40 mm/56-caliber machine guns, which were either single- or double-barreled. This was also a multipurpose weapon but focused on aircraft. (Antiaircraft guns were known as ack-ack guns.) Fed with two four-round clips the loader had to load continuously, the gun had trainer and pointer seats and was hand-operated. It was manned by a five-man crew. A chest-high, steel splinter shield or gun tub surrounded the Bofors.

Small arms

To round out the complement, each patrol craft was equipped with Browning Automatic Rifles, Thompson machine guns, 30-caliber rifles, pistols, and grenades for those encounters of an intimate nature.

Normandy:
A Father's Ship and a Son's Curiosity

The mystery of the weaponry

According to the *General Information Book*, when commissioned, the *PC 552* had two three-inch/50-caliber guns, one fore and one aft. It had two 20 mm Oerlikons mounted on the chart house; two stern depth-charge release racks; and two K guns, one on each side.[16] This was confirmed on the information card completed when the ship was assigned to be decommissioned in 1946—so far, so good.

However, photos of the ship show a Bofors 40 mm/56-caliber machine gun where the aft three-inch/50-caliber gun was supposed to be (see image "*PC 552* salutes Normandy beaches" in chapter 12). Also, various contemporaneous reports seemed to imply additional 20 mm Oerlikons. Poring over multiple documents gave tantalizing hints but no clear picture. For example, the deck log entry for 23 August 1943 noted that new guns were taken aboard but does not identify them or explain why. Finally, the best answer came from the model of the *PC 552* built by Lt. Frank Pierce. There we see, definitively, a Bofors 40 mm/56-caliber machine gun aft in place of the aft three-inch gun. We also see *five* 20 mm Oerlikons—one on the pilot house, two on the chart house, and two on the main deck flanking the 40 mm Bofors.

As a final observation, the *PC 470* was commissioned two days after the *PC 552* with two three-inch guns, one fore and one aft. There was no mousetrap. In 1943, we know the *PC 470* replaced the aft three-inch gun with a 40 mm Bofors, and two mousetraps were installed.[17] The 40 mm Bofors was a more effective antiaircraft gun,

---

[16] *General Information Book for PCs 552–555*. Issued by the US Navy. Cover page missing (basically the ships' owner's manual). Source: National Archives and Records Administration (NARA), College Park, MD.

[17] W. Neil McBride, *When In All Ways Ready for the Sea* (St. Petersburg, FL: Attraction Center Publishing, 2009), p. 39.

and the mousetrap was a more effective antisubmarine weapon (compared to the ash cans). It seems the same thing happened to the *PC 552*.

The 20 mm on the pilot house is where Roland Stine got into a disagreement with a German ship; the aft guns are where Ted Guzda and Bill Kesnick stood back-to-back to fight the Germans on D-Day (see chapter 11). A mousetrap in the photo of the model is not visible, although it may be hidden by the gunnel. In a telephone conversation on 15 September 2017, Bill Kesnick verified the ship had two mousetraps forward, just where they should have been. It appears the sailors

Figure 17. Steel pennies
In an effort to save copper for the manufacture of ammunition casings, in 1943, the US Mint experimented with steel pennies. It didn't work out, as the pennies rusted, got stuck in vending machines because they were attracted by magnets, and were often mistaken for dimes. They remained in circulation until the mid-1960s, as most baby boomers fondly remember.

who processed the decommissioning paperwork never actually inspected the ship prior to decommissioning it.

Such is life: 24 officers and 198 men officially served on the *PC 552*. Many more were aboard her for transportation and other reasons. They all must have routinely tripped over those weapons and barked their shins and cursed them but never memorialized the weapons anywhere because *everyone* knew about them—everyone, that is, except the historians who would come some decades later to painstakingly reconstruct what was once common knowledge.

3
The Danger and the Times

Those of us who are the children of the World War II generation know a great deal about that war. We are often surprised to find succeeding generations have little understanding of what happened. After I published the first edition of this book, it became apparent to me that an overview of World War II would make this story clearer.

The United States, the United Kingdom, China, India, and (later) the Soviet Union and their associates were termed the Allies. Germany, Italy, and Japan and their associates were termed the Axis. From the United States' standpoint, the danger came from two directions.

Danger from the east: the Nazis (Fascists)

Nazi Germany was sweeping everything in its path. It looked like it had the United Kingdom on the ropes and was deep into Russia. Although most of the atrocities came to light only during the close of the war, the leaders of the United States knew Nazi Germany was a ruthless dictatorship that

Figure 18. An abandoned boy
Following a German aerial bombing of London, this child came home from playing to find his home gone and his father, mother, and brother dead under the rubble he is sitting on.
Photo by Toni Frissell. Source: http://rarehistoricalphotos.com.

27

would not hesitate to bathe millions in blood. Germany was a very powerful country with a strong economy, which could finance a major war. It had a professional, effective military and was a serious opponent. Italy sided with Germany, and the Allies watched country after country fall to the Nazis. To the east, Germany overran Czechoslovakia, Austria, Poland, half of Russia, and a host of smaller countries. To the west, Germany overran the Netherlands and Belgium and took out France with its colonies to the south in North Africa. The Battle of Britain began, and Germany was pounding the United Kingdom to its knees. US leaders worried that if the United Kingdom fell, the United States and Canada would be all alone to face a powerful Nazi Germany across the Atlantic. In fact, German U-boats already patrolled off the Atlantic coast of North and South America.

The Axis powers were well aware of

Figure 19. "Boogie Woogie Bugle Boy," by the Andrews Sisters

He was a famous trumpet man from out Chicago way
He had a boogie style that no one else could play
He was the top man at his craft
But then his number came up and he was gone with the draft
He's in the army now, a blowin' reveille
He's the boogie woogie bugle boy of Company B

The United States began to reluctantly gear up for war before Pearl Harbor. A peacetime draft was imposed in 1940, and this very popular song came out in January 1941.

The Andrews Sisters were perhaps one of the most popular women singing groups of all time. During World War II, they wore pseudo uniforms and did a lot of supportive entertaining of military personnel.
Source: coleypugtalksoldmovies.blogspot.com.

the United States' economic might. They had watched the United States enter World War I with almost nothing, only to see it turn out and transport hundreds of thousands of superbly trained and

equipped soldiers across the Atlantic. The Axis knew the American economic system could turn on a dime and outproduce everyone

Destroyer Reuben James sunk October 31

Figure 20. Stamp commemorating the USS *Reuben James*
Source: US Post Office

else. Therefore, key to the German World War II strategy was the conquering of Europe before the United States entered the war, to leave the United States, Canada, and the rest of the Americas to face a Fortress Europe alone.

The United States' approach was initially to quietly provide the Allies with weapons and supplies. The British were responsible for shepherding these materials across the Atlantic in the face of the German U-boats, as the United States was not officially at war. As that became untenable, the United States "lent" fifty destroyers to the United Kingdom to help convoy the merchant ships carrying the munitions. The United States did this as part of what became known as the Lend-Lease program, which was really just a ruse to supply the United Kingdom and the Soviet Union.

As that situation deteriorated, the United States convoyed merchant ships in its own right as far as Iceland, after which the British took over. In April 1941, the United Kingdom invaded and occupied Iceland to deny it to Germany, but the Royal Marines were replaced by US Marines at the request of both the United Kingdom and Iceland. An unofficial war was going on between the United States and Germany in the North Atlantic. Both sides were trying to be careful not to precipitate official war, but President Roosevelt finally ordered the US Navy to shoot German U-boats on sight on 11 September 1941[18] because of some damage inflicted on American warships. The most important US casualty prior to the United States' official entry into the war was the USS *Reuben James*, which was sunk by a German U-boat 31 October 1941 and lost all officers and ninety-two sailors.[19] Thus a quasi-war was fought between the United States and Germany with ships sunk and Americans dying lonely deaths in the freezing gales of the North Atlantic during most of 1941. If the United States had needed an excuse to enter World War II, it had plenty.

Danger from the west: the

> George Bush Sr., the forty-third US president, was the youngest fighter pilot in the US Navy during World War II. He volunteered for combat against his father's wishes and participated in a bombing run in September 1944 on Chichi Jima Island, during which he and nine of his comrades were shot down and landed in the water. He ditched away from the island and—vomiting, bleeding from a head wound, delirious, and crying—was picked up by a submarine. His comrades ditched closer to the island and made it to land. There, after much suffering, they were slaughtered, and the Japanese ate their livers and thighs in a cannibalistic ceremony. Charles Laurence, "George HW Bush narrowly escaped comrades' fate of being killed and eaten by Japanese captors," *The Telegraph*, 06 February 2017.

[18] Franklin D. Roosevelt, "Fireside Chat number 18," 11 September 1941. Accessed 04 July 2017. https://www.youtube.com/watch?v=fUWJX-j1xws.

[19] "Rescue 44 Men of Sunken Destroyer," *Boston Post*, 01 November 1941.

Japanese

On the Pacific side, the Japanese were building their empire. The Japanese government was split into various competing political factions, including its army and navy.

The army had gone on a particularly brutal conquering spree in China, during which Japanese soldiers routinely held contests in which the participants raced to see who could decapitate the most people in a fixed period. We may still see photos of Japanese soldiers bayonetting Chinese babies and throwing them in boiling water. They took joy in using prisoners for bayonet practice and participated in ritual cannibalism.

When the Japanese conquered the Chinese capital of Nanking, they burned most of the city, killed between 260,000 and 350,000 people, raped between 20,000 and 80,000 women and girls, and cut off their breasts and nailed people to walls.[20] This is just one instance of a routine attitude the Japanese had toward all peoples in their power, and their wanton cruelty will never be understandable. As hard as this is to believe, they exceeded the Nazis in terms of cruelty and certainly killed as many people. Americans do

> Baby boomers grew up "knowing" that carrots would improve eyesight. What they didn't know was that this was purely British propaganda. During the Battle of Britain, German bombers began to come across the Channel under the cover of darkness to evade the Royal Air Force fighters. In response, the British equipped some fighters with radar to intercept the bombers. To explain the uncanny interceptions without revealing the use of radar, the British explained their pilots were eating a lot of carrots, which improved their eyesight. A whole story built around John "Cat's Eyes" Cunningham, a bona fide British ace, attributed his success to carrots.
> K. Annabelle Smith, "A WWII Propaganda Campaign Popularized the Myth That Carrots Help You See in the Dark," *The Smithsonian,* 13 August 2013.

---

[20] *Newsweek* Staff, "Exposing the Rape of Nanking," *Newsweek,* 30 November 1997.

not properly appreciate the horror. Many Chinese (and Koreans) hate the Japanese with a passion to this day, and they resent Americans who tell them to "get over it."

The Japanese bought American steel, oil, and rubber to support their war efforts in China. Understandably, the United States wanted no part of this and eventually refused to

Figure 21. Decapitation contest
This celebratory article from the 13 December 1937 edition of the *Tokyo Nichi Nichi Shimbun* lightheartedly follows a contest between two Japanese lieutenants to see who could chop the most heads in an hour.
Source: Pinterest

continue the sale of such goods. Without these supplies, the Japanese had a choice of pulling out from China or doubling down. The Japanese army doubled down for internal political reasons and so eyed the natural resources of various regional European colonies that were defenseless because the European powers were distracted by war. The Imperial Japanese Navy, which actually had to fight the United States in the event of war, opposed this but was powerless to stop the war faction. The only power left in the Pacific that could challenge the Empire of Japan was the United States, so Japanese officials began to paint the United States as the archenemy. To this day some people in Japan claim the United States started the war by refusing to sell Japan the materials needed to continue their war effort in China.

Normandy:
A Father's Ship and a Son's Curiosity

As bizarre as this seems, the Japanese knew they could never win a war against the United States. The Japanese had spies in Hawaii and the continental United States, and one of their tasks was to determine the United States' industrial capacity.[21] Additionally, the Japanese military also played out numerous war games. The answer was always the same: Japan could run riot for a few years, but the United States would eventually massively outproduce Japan, and defeat was inevitable.[22] This was understood in the highest circles, yet the Japanese still bombed Pearl Harbor and conquered the Philippines. Their thinking was to provide such a crushing first strike against the United States that the United States would just give up. It didn't happen that way.

The United States' approach was to avoid conflict with Japan at all costs so it could focus on the real threat, Nazi Germany. Although US leadership never felt the issue with Japan on its own would be in doubt, the United States was deeply concerned about Nazi Germany.

Thus, the danger

To the east, Eurasia and Africa were dominated by a ruthless German power, with menacing German U-boats patrolling the Atlantic coast; to the west, China, Indochina, and the Pacific were dominated by Japan, with the navy of the Empire of Japan off the Pacific coast. Both enemies had shown their utter disdain for any sort of moderation and, if successful, were likely to go after the United States to force their philosophies on that country in time.

---

[21] Craig Nelson, *Pearl Harbor: From Infamy to Greatness* (New York: Scribner, 2016), 127–128.

[22] Ibid., 56–57.

While the United States was unofficially at war with Nazi Germany, the United States' hand was forced into open war by the attack on Pearl Harbor on 07 December 1941. After that attack, the American people supported the war enthusiastically. Germany helped this process by declaring war on the United States after the Japanese attack on Pearl Harbor, and the mighty American economy rumbled into gear.[23]

The American wartime strategy

The American strategy was straightforward. It sought to stop the Japanese and slowly turn them and keep pressure on them while focusing most of the attention

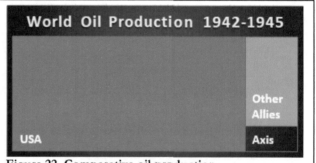

Figure 22. Comparative oil production

Oil is the lifeblood of warfare. During this period, the United States produced 6 billion barrels; all other Allies produced 1.1 billion barrels; and the combined Axis produced 0.3 billion barrels, including synthetic oil. Source: John Ellis, *World War II: A Statistical Survey*, (1993) Table 81.

on Nazi Germany—the goal was to take Germany out before it took out the United Kingdom and Soviet Union. The United States caught wind of the Nazi project to create an atom bomb and started the

---

[23] John R. Cary spent his formative years during the Great Depression. He wrote with awe to his mother about something he saw in the army. He repeated this several times after the war, each time with the wonder still fresh: In his company, after each meal, the soldiers threw away enough food to feed his family for a week. And a lot of it was meat!

Manhattan Project to beat the Nazis to the punch. Fortunately for Germany, the Allies conquered Germany using conventional means before the United States finished the atom bomb.

The United States played to its strength. The war was a production and logistics problem for the United States, something no one else did better. It

Figure 23. Pistol Packin' Mamas
Frances Green, Margaret Kirchner, Ann Waldner, and Blanche Osborn leave their *B-17* bomber, *Pistol Packin' Mama*, at Lockbourne Air Force Base in Ohio.
A shortage of male pilots caused the military to establish the Women Airforce Service Pilots (WASP) to fly bombers and aircraft to where they could be sent overseas.
Source: NARA.

outproduced all the other combatants combined and supplied all allies. The United States vastly exceeded its World War I record in terms of quantity and speed.

The European theater

The first order of business for the European theater, the ultimate theater of the *PC 552*, was to produce antisubmarine ships and planes and the sailors and airmen to fight them. The US Navy and Coast Guard took on the U-boats and cleared them from the Atlantic shore with British and Canadian assistance. They then stockpiled men and equipment until they crossed the Atlantic, fighting U-boats all the way, to clear North Africa with the British Empire (including Canada, Australia, New Zealand, South Africa, and others). Then the western Allies hopped across to Sicily and began the campaign up the Italian peninsula until the Italians quit.

Finally, while the Russians, supplied by the Americans, pounded the Nazis from the east, the United States and Britain pounded the Nazis from the skies. The Allies stockpiled war material in England until making the jump across to France on D-Day to fight their way to the heart of Germany to meet the Russians.[24]

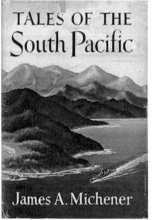

Figure 24. *Tales of the South Pacific*

A bestselling book published in 1947, this is a touching medley of loosely connected stories of World War II. The story about the tight-lipped military man from Down Under who finally breaks down after drinking to give his heartfelt thanks to the Yanks for protecting his wife and family back home is moving.

The Pacific theater

In the Pacific, it was largely a navy war. The Japanese had surrounded their conquests by a perimeter of islands, which had to be taken down one by one. The Americans fought a delaying action in the Philippines, then rushed to protect its last allies, Australia and New Zealand, to prevent them from being knocked out of the war. The United States stopped the Japanese advance at the Aleutians and Midway Island, then began the relentless pressure, hopping from one island to the next, punching a hole in the Japanese perimeter and ignoring the islands on either side, ever closer to the Japanese homeland. Before

---

[24] Deep in a Central American jungle, Specialist Miller repeated to me the story his father told him about encountering German jets for the first time. He was inside Germany and racing in his tank toward the enemy. He was sitting up in the hatch on the turret when a *whoosh* flew over his head and then was long gone. Only later did the machine gun bullets rain down on him.

the invasion of the Japanese homeland could begin, the Americans finished developing the atomic bomb and dropped two on Japan. As soon as the Soviets noted the dropping of the atomic bombs, the Soviet Union immediately attacked Japan in Manchuria, and Japan surrendered to the United States as the best choice.

The Soviet Union and Nazi Germany

In 1939, Nazi Germany and the Soviet Union signed a nonaggression pact in an iniquitous plan to divide eastern Europe between them. Poland was destroyed and shared between the two. They destroyed other countries, also. In 1941, in a display of honor among thieves, Germany attacked the Soviet Union. Under Joseph Stalin, the Soviet Union committed as many atrocities as the others, but the enemy of the Axis became the friend of the Allies. President Roosevelt had to clean up Stalin's reputation in the States for practical reasons and referred to him as "Uncle Joe." He was not an uncle most would have wanted.

The (nonexistent) conspiracy

The United States had been deeply isolationist and had not invested much in the military for traditional reasons—historically, the United States has kept a small military—and because of the Great Depression. The American people had experienced World War I and had no taste for involvement in another war that many did not think was their business. From time to time, we hear conspiracy theories about how Roosevelt (or somebody) in the United States arranged for Pearl Harbor to happen so that Roosevelt could convince the people of the United States to enter the war. Careful review of the evidence refutes this. The truth seems to be the world was sitting on a powder keg and there was no need to allow an attack. The trick was not to precipitate an attack—that would have been very easy—but to prevent an official war until the United States was ready and then to fight initially against only Germany to keep the United Kingdom and the Soviets in the fight. The United States was already unofficially in a war with Germany and needed no justification. Prior to Pearl Harbor, Japan had already attacked American ships and killed Americans, which the American government glossed over to prevent a war.

One such example occurred on 12 December 1937. During the Rape of Nanking, Japanese imperial forces bombed and sank the USS *Panay*, which was evacuating American civilians and was anchored twenty miles upstream in the Yangtze River. The attack was a surprise. The Japanese strafed the survivors attempting to escape in lifeboats. After making it to shore, the survivors cowered in the swamp in knee-deep mud to hide from the Japanese planes circling overhead. Four died, and scores were injured. Four years later, almost to the day, the Japanese attacked Pearl Harbor the same way.[25]

As President Roosevelt himself said to a firebrand, "It is terribly important for the control of the Atlantic for us to keep peace in the Pacific. I simply have not got enough Navy to go round—and every little episode in the Pacific means fewer ships in the Atlantic."[26]

The roles of the US Marines and the US Army

There are a lot of misunderstandings surrounding World War II. One is about the roles of the US Army and the US Marines. The US Marines are the land extension of the US Navy. They have always specialized in limited expeditionary engagements and rely on the US Navy for all their support. The navy provides their logistics and

---

[25] "Suddenly and Deliberately Attacked! The Story of the Panay Incident," The USS Panay Memorial Website, Accessed 25 March 2018, http://usspanay.org/attacked.shtml.

[26] FDR's response to Interior Secretary Harold Ickes's letter of 23 June 1941.

major artillery and air support. Even their medics are navy personnel called "corpsmen." If one has a limited objective, particularly one accessible from the sea, such as an island, call in the US Marines. This is why the marines were chosen for the island-hopping campaign in the Pacific war (supported by twenty-two army divisions). Marine strength peaked at about six divisions during World War II.[27] As the Pacific War was mostly a naval war, the marines' purpose was to acquire islands to be used as naval ports and provide runways for the army to bomb Japan.

In contrast, the US Army is a self-contained force, responsible for all its own logistics and support. During World War II, even the air force was part of the army, then called the US Army Air Corps. The air force became a separate force only after World War II. If you want something—such as a Nazi army— truly obliterated on a massive scale and left a smoking ruin, call in the US

Figure 25. Expert Marksmanship Badge
Both the US Marines and the US Army focus on riflery first. On the left is an expert marine badge; on the right is an expert army badge.

Army. The army peaked at ninety-two divisions.[28] This is why the army was chosen for the European campaign. The army gained enormous experience in amphibious assaults in North Africa; Italy; southern France; and the granddaddy of them all, D-Day.

---

[27] Marine Corps University, "Battle Honors of the Six Marine Divisions in WWII," Official Marine Corps website. Accessed 06 September 2017. www.usmcu.edu/historydivision/battle-honors-six-marine-divisions-wwii.

[28] Excluding the twenty ghost divisions created for subterfuge purposes.

In my experience, having served as an infantry soldier with both, the US Marines emphasize a stricter obedience to orders and a doctrine of direct assault, while the US Army emphasizes initiative and decision making at the soldier level (those on the scene). When faced with an obstacle, the US Marines tend to frontally attack it. The US Army would rather rain artillery and air strikes on it, then look for a means to outflank it. Both soldiers and marines are riflemen first, and both deserve our respect, but each has its own doctrine suitable to its specific purpose and should be honored. A grunt is always a grunt.

Artillery

Much has been said about the innovative German blitzkrieg with its use of armor, and much of that is correct. Those who like to feel smug about how their country performed compared to how France quickly fell forget that their country had the good fortune to not be next to Germany. The French army's contribution was honorable.

However, in the years between World War I and World War II, while the German army focused on armor tactics, the US Army focused on artillery tactics pioneered by Orlando Ward, who liked to observe monkeys in the national zoo because, as he said, it helped him understand the primates in the War Department. The ability to order an artillery strike was given to the small unit level (lieutenants, backed up by NCOs) through radios called walkie-talkies. Moreover, local artillery batteries were tied together by radio to Fire Direction Control centers so that all artillery in range could be directed on target by that same small unit in minutes instead of the usual six hours. The results were devastating.[29] One observation—repeated so many times it is impossible to provide the original attribution—was that when the Germans opened up their artillery, the Allies took

[29] Rick Atkinson, *An Army at Dawn* (New York: Henry Holt and Company, 2002).

cover; when the British artillery unleashed its fury, the Germans took cover; and when the Americans pulled the lanyards on their artillery, *everybody* took cover. Many German generals had no opinion of the ability of the American fighting man. When asked why, they said they never saw them fight—they *couldn't* see them through all the explosions.

FIND YOUR WAR JOB
In Industry – Agriculture – Business

Figure 26. Women in the workforce
Source: Office of War Information Second World War Industrial Employment Poster, OWI No. 55 by George Rapp.

Socially

Women

Most people know that the men going to war caused a shortage of workers required to build the engines of war. Traditional male roles had to be filled by women, and at first there was pushback from all sides; however, the government moved to encourage women to enter traditionally male jobs. "Rosie the Riveter" became a song in 1942 and a Hollywood movie in 1944. Women were encouraged by such taglines as "Can you use an electric mixer? If so, you can learn to operate a drill."[30] Six million women joined the workforce.[31]

Culture

It is impossible to listen to the American music of World War II without sensing the raw energy and confidence bubbling just below the surface. This is the music of a people who were going to win a war! People such as Glenn Miller and his band, the Andrews Sisters, Duke Ellington, and a host of others created clearly inspirational sounds. Some of the lyrics are timeless and should be heard today.

---

[30] Lee Kennett, *For the Duration…: the United States Goes to War, Pearl Harbor-1942* (New York: Scribner, 1985).

[31] Ursula Wood, "We Can Do It!," *New Moon* 12, no. 1 (2004).

Listen to such instrumentals as "American Patrol" or songs such as "Don't Sit Under the Apple Tree (With Anyone Else But Me)" and see if you can't still feel the vibrations of that past. The dancing is the same: confident and energetic and a marvel to watch. What was often not publicly recognized but was often privately understood was that black American culture strongly underpinned the music and the dance of the times, the boogie-woogie jive.

Integration

The American military was officially segregated, and blacks were officially relegated to support roles such as stevedores and messmen. However, as often happens when the chips are down, such distinctions evaporated in the face of common danger. This is a measurable phenomenon going back to the American Revolution.

It is no accident Martin Luther King Jr. et al. came along twenty years after the war. During World War II, a white captain and a black sergeant became simply a captain and a sergeant. Blacks eventually made it to frontline positions, and their

Figure 27. *United We Win*
Photograph by Alexander Liberman, 1943.
Printed by the Government Printing Office for the War Manpower Commission
Source: NARA Still Picture Branch
(NWDNS-44-PA-370).

effectiveness was noted. Black American artillery units were created and deployed to the front, and black soldiers were quietly assigned to previously all-white infantry units. It seemed to military leadership that even black people could stop a bullet, a privilege previously exclusive to nonblack people. White people noted and respected this at the time. There were certainly problems, but some official films of the times shortly after World War II show whites and blacks in uniform in mixed groups without any issues or even apparent awareness. They had made it back together. They had drunk from the same canteen. The military was officially desegregated in 1948, but it is apparent to the observant that this had been happening unofficially before then.

And now back to our ship

All this was the unknown future for the crew of the *PC 552*, which was launched near the end of that initial stage of the Battle of Atlantic, where it immediately began to attack suspected U-boats. The crew had no knowledge of how the future would turn out.

4

Tactics

There are those who say combat consists of long periods of abject boredom interspersed with moments of sheer terror. The men of the *PC 552* knew this. Throughout most of 1942 and 1943, they were the hunters, not the hunted. They convoyed ships and launched attacks against suspected enemy submarines. Once across the Atlantic, they became more of a target in their own right, particularly on D-Day. As many were told, the quickest way to get back home to Chicago was through Berlin, a thought most internalized.

Patrol craft were verified to have destroyed only fifteen submarines[32] and torpedo-type craft and twenty-four enemy aircraft during World War II, which sounds paltry but misses the point. The mission of patrol craft was not to destroy submarines; it was to protect convoys. The goal was to get men and war material across the seas and up to the beaches, and in that, the patrol craft served admirably. The typical German Class-VII U-boat (the German submarine workhorse) cost $2.25 million[33] to build in terms of 1943 dollars; cost even more to

---

[32] As time passes, we learn more. *PC 566* was finally credited with the sinking of a German U-boat forty-five miles south of the Mississippi Delta in 2012. The skipper reported the sinking of the U-boat on 30 July 1942, but he was not believed, as neither the crew nor the ship had been trained in submarine warfare yet. Oil company divers verified the kill much later. Jon Harper, "Navy admits error, honors World War II captain's bravery in sinking of U-boat," *The Stars and Stripes*, 19 December 2014.

[33] Michel Poirier, "Results of the German and American Submarine Campaigns of World War II," Chief of Naval Operations-Submarine Warfare Division, US Navy, 20 Oct 1999.

crew, provision, and deploy; and carried only twelve torpedoes.[34] In essence, "deploying a torpedo" to the mid-Atlantic region was a very expensive proposition, and torpedoes were not to be wasted on nonstrategic targets such as patrol craft. Thus, enemy submarines avoided patrol craft and attempted to sneak past them to get to the strategic targets, the merchant ships.

Another reason for the lack of verified kills is that it was hard to verify the destruction of a submarine. Submarines were underwater, and they sank when destroyed. Crew members usually surmised destruction had occurred from floating wreckage, oil slicks, and other signs. Submarines quickly learned to feign destruction by jettisoning life preservers; fuel; and even bodies, if available. For example, *PC 552* believed it made contact with an enemy submarine on 21 September 1942 and observed dirty water after attacking. This was repeated the following day, when crew members observed an oil slick. There was no

Figure 28. The men's Victory Suit
Both men and women wore what was called the Victory Suit. In the case of women, it was the elimination of nonutilitarian frills. In the case of men, it was the elimination of the extra pair of pants and the vest. Vests did not return to fashion until the 1980s, and then only briefly.
Source:
http://www.gurjotnewyork.com/blog/the-history-of-the-suit-world-war-ii-and-the-victory-suit/

[34] Naval Intelligence Division 08408/43 (December 1943). CB04051 (90) "*U 470*" "*U 533*" Interrogation of Survivors. Admiralty, SWI (UK).

definitive proof of destruction of a U-boat, but such destruction was suspected.

Convoy protection

Patrol craft were stationed at the outside of a zigzagging convoy, where they screened their portion of the convoy perimeter, patrolling back and forth in a faster zigzag pattern. This made it hard for submarines to torpedo a merchant ship, because the patrol craft would get in the way. Ship crew members listened for possible enemy submarines with sonar, and when they suspected they'd found one, they came to General Quarters and immediately launched depth charges in the suspected location. The ship then traveled a pattern, going back and forth, launching depth charges the whole time.

The helmsman gripped the helm so tight his knuckles turned white as he listened for the commands barked from the skipper. The skipper constantly imagined a three-dimensional model of the ocean in which he mentally mapped where the submarine was going in its attempt to break contact, shouting course changes based on his guesses. Where would he go if he were a submarine? Subs often made sudden right-angle turns, which the patrol craft could determine because they lost contact. The only thing the skipper could do was flip a coin; did the sub go left or right? Sailors frantically busted knuckles using wrenches to set the ash cans to explode at the prescribed depths, then kicked them off the stern of the ship to a resounding splash, silence for a while, then an unnatural mound rising from the fathoms below, accompanied by a hellish shock wave.

During this time, the submarine ran silently and deeply, attempting to change course radically, hoping the ship lost contact.

Because of the Doppler effect, a patrol craft could determine a U-boat's approximate heading through sonar. A U-boat coming toward the patrol craft would have an increasingly higher pitch, and a U-boat heading away from the patrol craft would have an increasingly lower pitch.

Thus, the game of cat and mouse: The submarine attempted to sneak past the patrol craft to torpedo a merchant ship, and the patrol craft listened for the submarine to kill it. Once contact was lost, the patrol craft went back to screening the convoy. That was its job—not killing submarines.

PC 552 protected numerous convoys up and down the east coast and the Caribbean, as well as Convoy *UGS 29* to the United Kingdom, as part of Task Force 69. It also screened for the Battle of Normandy fleet. During this period, *PC 552* made contact with suspected enemy submarines many times, vigorously attacking them on each occasion. It was credited with only one kill on 15 May 1943, but that was a judgment call, just as it was a judgment call that the other engagements did not result in kills.

Surface battles

Surface battles were different. Surprisingly, a typical enemy submarine outgunned a patrol craft. Thus, if a submarine wished to engage a patrol craft, it surfaced and began firing its deck gun, which had a longer range than the patrol craft's gun and was more powerful. The patrol craft's tactic was to race toward the submarine as quickly as possible and ram it before the submarine could bring its gun to bear. The patrol craft's hull was stronger and would crack the submarine's conning tower. This was actually done only once, and it was successful.

Although the *PC 552* suffered air attacks numerous times, it had only one documented surface-to-surface engagement with a German E-boat 06 and 07 February 1945. In this case, *PC 552* outgunned the

47

target, and the engagement consisted of a race. Ultimately, the German E-boat got away. Radioman First Class Roland "Nick" Stine remembered another one, which was not officially documented. His reminiscences are in "Personal Experiences" (chapter 11).

Amphibious landings

These tactics changed when it came to amphibious landings, as at Normandy. Because of their speed, shallow draft, and maneuverability, patrol craft were ideal forward observers for the navy as it attempted to land soldiers and materiel in attack. They were often the navy ships closest to the enemy, making observations and policing the invasion waves. As such, they became targets of primary importance. In warfare, a primary goal is to destroy the enemy's leaders and communication to inspire confusion and lack of confidence. The patrol craft were certainly communication; thus, they were primary targets.

Now, let's meet the *PC 552*.

5
The *PC 552* Is Launched

The wider world

When the *PC 552* was launched in February 1942, the Americans had just initiated a very successful raid on the Japanese in the Marshall and Gilbert Islands. The Japanese lost one carrier, a cruiser, and a number of other ships. Singapore was still holding out, although it was cut off and surrounded. The British got the bad end of an engagement with the

Figure 29. The front page of the *New York Times* for 13 February 1942 Source: Monterey Public Library, Monterey, CA.

German Fleet, and the US Republican leadership called for its own war plans.

The original cost of *PC 552* was $625,000. It was built by the Sullivan Dry Dock and Repair Co. in Brooklyn, New York, and was originally scheduled for completion 12 November 1941. The keel was laid 20 May 1941.

Launch of the USS *PC 552*

PC 552 was launched the evening of 13 February 1942 from the Sullivan shipyard in Brooklyn, New York. This was the first night launch of the Third Naval District, a change made so work could begin on a sister ship, *PC 555*, immediately. The navy considered night launches risky, because of the lack of visibility. This was a wartime exigency.

About two thousand people attended the launch, roughly half of whom were the workers who had built *PC 552*. Rear Admiral Adolphus Andrews, commandant of the Third Naval District and commander of the North Atlantic coastal frontier, said,

Figure 30. USS *PC 552* is christened by Miss Grace Finley
The Sullivan Dry Dock and Repair Company in Brooklyn, New York, 13 February 1942. Source: Naval History and Heritage Command.

"Everything connected with this war must be on a 24-hour basis. These night launchings should be the most common occurrence in the world. Not a minute should be wasted in getting out the ships and planes and supplies of every sort that are needed on our many fighting fronts."[35]

The wind was bitingly cold as Rev. Arthur R. Cummings, pastor of the Church of the Resurrection in Richmond Hill, blessed the vessel. With him was Rev. William J. Farrell, port chaplain in Brooklyn.

Grace Finley, age sixteen, a junior at Richmond Hill High School and the daughter of Leslie H. Finley, office manager of the Sullivan Company, smashed a bottle of champagne against *PC 552*, which plunged violently into the water. Miss Finley was bundled up in a

---

[35] "2,000 See Launching of Submarine Chaser," *Brooklyn Eagle*, 14 February 1942.

thick coat against the bitter wind blowing off the waters of New York Harbor. The ship was launched sideways with a resounding splash while the men on the ship held on for dear life. The keel of the next ship was laid immediately.[36] The US Navy issued a press release, and the launch was reported in the *New York Times*.

The ship was then fitted out at the New York Building Yard on 16 March 1942. The schedule for USS *PC 522*'s completion was extended first to 22 June 1942, then to 30 June 1942. On 09 July 1942, the navy authorized the ship's acceptance, subject to further trials. Preliminary trials were completed 17 July 1942, and the ship was accepted 27 July 1942 and commissioned.[37] The crew boarded 29–30 July 1942.

The neighborhood

The neighborhood today is very different from how it was in those times. The Sullivan Dry Dock and Repair Company sat at the end of

Do with less— so they'll have enough!

RATIONING GIVES YOU YOUR FAIR SHARE

Figure 31. Rationing
Rationing was introduced so that all Americans, regardless of wealth, had access to the basics. "Red Stamp" rationing covered all meats, butter, fat, and oils, and with some exceptions, cheese. "Blue Stamp" rationing covered canned, bottled, frozen fruits and vegetables, plus juices and dry beans, and such processed foods as soups, baby food and ketchup. Tires and gasoline were also rationed and Americans supplemented their diets from Victory Gardens, vegetables grown at home.
Publisher: Washington, D.C. Distributed by Division of Public Inquiries, Office of War Information, U.S. G.P.O. 1943.

---

[36] Ibid.

[37] US Navy, "*PC 552* Vessel History Card." Source: NARA.

Twenty-Third Street in the Tebo Basin in Brooklyn, New York. Judging from numerous photos, it was a very busy place then; it is a quiet neighborhood now.

In the morning, men trudged to work at the end of each street, clutching their lunch pails as the factory whistles blew. Wives sent the children to school and returned to their work. At the factories

Figure 32. Present launch site
This is the modern site where the ship was launched at the end of Twenty-Third Street in Brooklyn (as of July 2015). There is now a power station there, and it is a very quiet residential neighborhood.

and shipyards, metal clanged and blowtorches flared. In the evening, the whistles blew again, and the men trudged back to baths and dinner. The neighborhood was then a working-class Polish-Catholic neighborhood with row houses and local restaurants, and traces of the flavor remain. No locals seem to remember the business that

went on during the war. The Virgin Mary still gazes sorrowfully on parishioners as she did on those people of long ago, but priests at the local church where many of the locals must have worshipped have no memory of the times.

The Sullivan Dry Dock and Repair Company

There is now no physical trace of the Sullivan Dry Dock and Repair Company, a onetime major Brooklyn employer.

Figure 33. US Supreme Court opinion

Normandy:
A Father's Ship and a Son's Curiosity

Ironically, Sullivan's primary and lasting legacy was to be based in a labor dispute that made legal history.

As war loomed, Congress passed the Selective Training and Service Act of 1940. The act called for a worker's seniority to accrue while he served in the military. It also called for military veterans to have priority to get their jobs back upon their return (assuming an honorable discharge) and not be subject to employment "discharge" without cause for one year.

Abraham Fishgold had joined Sullivan as a welder in 1942. In 1943 he was drafted into the army. He was subsequently honorably discharged and returned to work at Sullivan. Mr. Fishgold was laid off for nine days, while a nonveteran with greater seniority was not laid off. Mr. Fishgold asked to be paid for the nine days ($94.60), because he should not have been discharged. The court ruled against Mr. Fishgold, on the basis that a layoff was not a discharge. The Local 13 of the Industrial Union of Marine and Shipbuilding Workers of America opposed Mr. Fishgold, and Sullivan felt it needed to support the union. Briefs were filed as *amici curiae* by the AFL, by the Railway Labor Executives' Association, by the CIO, and by other labor unions in support of Local 13—all very powerful unions.

The unions were strongly opposed to giving preference to a person returning from the war over a worker with seniority. According to experts testifying before a Senate committee on the matter, the Supreme Court ruling directly resulted in many veterans losing their jobs to nonveterans with greater seniority.[38]

---

[38] Andrew J. Huebner, *The Warrior Image: Soldiers in American Culture from World War II to the Vietnam Era* (Chapel Hill, NC: University of North Carolina Press, 2008).

This is Sullivan's lasting legacy. Very little is remembered about the Sullivan Dry Dock and Repair Company today or the warships it launched; what *is* remembered is that it figured prominently in a US Supreme Court decision concerning the right (or not) of a serviceman to get his job back with seniority intact after returning from the war. Its precedent is still routinely cited today.

Grace Finley

Miss Finley was locally prominent for a while, mentioned in the local society pages, and then disappeared. We can only speculate why, but it seems her father and four other Sullivan executives pled guilty in the Brooklyn federal court to charges of defrauding the government of $100,000. Her father was sentenced to nine months in prison and fined $1,000 as the least one involved. It must have been a horrendous time for her: one moment she was a prominent socialite launching a ship, and the next she was the daughter of a man vilified and sentenced to prison. When her father

Figure 34. Christening platform
At night at the Sullivan Dry Dock and Repair Company, Brooklyn, New York, 13 February 1942. Note the searchlight "spotlighting" the christening platform. Source: Naval History and Heritage Command.

was sentenced, Ms. Finley was a senior in high school. We can only imagine the emotions flying in her home at night while this was going on.

What the truth is, we don't know. Sullivan pumped out a lot of craft under enormous pressure in a time of labor and material shortages. The ships served well all over the Pacific and the Atlantic without complaint. There must have been temptations to hurry the process in the fog of the moment, which later could be misunderstood with perfect hindsight. District attorneys then were political animals, as they are now. Miss Finley should be best remembered as one of the many faces who launched a thousand ships, and we hope she had a fulfilling life.

Completion

After launch, the ship was fitted out in the historic New York Naval Shipyard (NYNS), also known as the Brooklyn Shipyard. As such, the *PC 552* was only the latest expression of US naval history. The shipyard was originally built in 1801 at the behest of Alexander Hamilton, among others, to protect American shipping from British and French aggression. Robert Fulton's steamship frigate was built there, and the ironclad USS *Monitor* was armored nearby. The battleship USS *Missouri*, the deck of which was the site of Japan's surrender on 02 September 1945, was also built there. The *PC 552* was a part of that heritage.

Now we meet the new crew members of the *PC 552*.

6

The Officers and Crew

The initial crew boarded the USS *PC 552* on 29–30 July 1942. The officers and senior noncommissioned officers boarded on 29 July, and the remainder of the crew boarded on 30 July and settled in for the first time. World War II navy slang referred to an original crew member as a "plank owner."[39]

In the wider world

Elsewhere on that first day, the US Supreme Court decided whether eight German spies who had been landed by a U-boat in Florida and on Long Island were subject to a military tribunal or entitled to a civilian trial. The eight had landed and buried their military equipment in the sand, then donned civilian clothes. Although the FBI under Herbert Hoover took credit for a masterful breaking-up of an espionage ring, the reality is that the spies were caught because one member had a change of heart and contacted the FBI. They had $172,000 and were tasked with destroying aluminum plants, canal locks, and railroad facilities: the plan was called "Operation Pastorius." At the heart of the judicial discussion was what exactly was an "unlawful enemy

Figure 35. Explosives disguised as lumps of coal Found with German spies. Source: NARA.

---

[39] W. Neil McBride, *When In All Ways Ready for the Sea* (St. Petersburg, FL: Attraction Center Publishing, 2009).

combatant" and what was a "theater of war." The court decided the defendants were subject to a military tribunal as an act of war, and six were eventually hanged as spies and saboteurs. The other two received long prison terms that were commuted after the war, and they were deported. This case held important precedent years later during the war in Afghanistan in the beginning of the twenty-first century.

Crewing the ship

The initial official complement of a PC during World War II was fifty-five enlisted men and four commissioned officers. The initial number of officers and men for the PCs commissioned by the US Navy was almost twenty-four thousand, yet a total of fifty thousand actually served, due to transfers, hospitalizations, and other factors.[40] Over time this was increased so that a typical complement was about sixty enlisted men and five officers. *PC 552* was no different.

The US Navy began a crash course to create sailors from the raw material of earnest, young men. Former heavyweight boxing champion George Tunney headed this initiative, which the

A yellow bird
with a yellow bill
Was sittin' on
my window sill
I lured him in
with crumbs of bread
And then I smashed (stomp)
his flamin' head

The moral of
The story is,
To get some head
You need some bread

An Army marching cadence. The sergeant called out the verse, and the unit repeated it. Instead of "flaming," another word was used. In some circles, it has become fashionable to criticize these teachings, but they provided the mind-set needed to make it back home. Mamas: your little boys are now American fighting men. Papas: you always quietly knew but never told Mama.

---

[40] Wm. J. Veigele, *PC Patrol Craft of World War II* (Santa Barbara, CA: Astral Publishing, 1998), 277.

navy called the "Tunney fish program." Tunney was tasked with finding athletes and high school coaches and transforming them into a cadre of boot camp instructors to turn the new recruits into sailors. They were known as Tunney fish[41] and given the rate of Chief Petty Officer, the navy equivalent of a First Sergeant.

This was a very serious rank, particularly for someone with no navy knowledge. But they did their job, cranking out sailors as if on an assembly line. A few years later, as the assembly line was in full throttle, their roles were taken on by professional boot camp instructors. The Tunney fish were assigned to ships, and one can't help but wonder how these highly ranked individuals with no knowledge of ships or the navy fared aboard ships for the first time.

In New York, the sailors gathered at Pier 92 to wait to be assigned to a ship. Pier 92 was where the luxury liners used to dock but was converted into housing. Men slept in iron cots stacked five high, and the bottom floor had a big shower room next to the offices and machine shops. In an attempt to prevent foot rot, the men laid newspapers on the floor; these quickly turned into

Figure 36. Stacy Stine Cary at Pier 92 in New York
The pier where the crews waited to be assigned their ships is now a major New York fashion venue (as of March 2018).

---

[41] Douglas L. Roberts, *Rustbucket 7* (Newcastle, ME: Mill Pond Press, 1995), 4.

ankle-deep mush until replaced.[42] It was a very loud place with metal clanging, harried messengers arriving and going, and little privacy.

There was clearly confusion as the *PC 552* was crewed. Almost as soon as the ships were crewed, there was churn. This happened for a variety of reasons. For one, health care was much more precarious in those days: antibiotics were a new concept, and diagnostic tools were not as effective. Many diseases for which a patient is now quickly diagnosed, treated, and sent home from the doctor's office required lengthy hospital stays then. When the patient was discharged, often his ship had sailed, and he had to be transferred. Another reason was that in this era of rapid mobilization, experienced sailors were highly prized. There was an ego factor about serving on a "real" ship, such as a carrier or a battleship. A sailor who had served on a patrol craft for a few months was now an "experienced" sailor and was often enticed to a larger ship. Patrol craft were initially built to fill the gap of enough destroyers. As destroyer escorts (DE) came off the production line, experienced PC crew members would be rotated to the destroyer escorts and new sailors would be assigned to the patrol craft. PCs were notorious for causing seasickness, and some people just never got over it.

Figure 37. The Stage Door Canteen
"Canteens" sprang up all over the country as a place for servicemen and women to hang out. The most famous one was in New York, where Lauren Bacall served doughnuts and danced with the men (as did other celebrities). Many sailors of the *PC 552* visited there.
Source: NARA

---

[42] W. Neil McBride, *When in All Ways Ready for Sea* (St. Petersburg, FL: Attraction Central Publishing, 2009), 20.

Some sailors just wished to serve with friends. There was plenty of "work" to go around.

One more factor was the US Navy's battles in the Pacific. After Pearl Harbor, the US Navy rushed to protect allies in the Pacific, resulting in inevitable casualties, including ships sunk. By May and June, just prior to the *PC 552*'s commissioning, the navy achieved stunning victories at Midway and the Coral Sea, but some additional American ships were sunk, most notably the aircraft carrier USS *Yorktown* with a crew of about 2,200 sailors. She didn't go down easily. Three Japanese aircraft carriers went down with her to serve her in Valhalla, and most of the sailors from the American ships were saved. These combat-experienced sailors were thus available to crew the new patrol craft being commissioned.

One such *PC 552* plank owner is Robert Benjamin Christensen, who was awarded the Silver Star for bravery. Christensen was on the *USS Langley*, the States' first aircraft carrier, which was torpedoed and sunk by the Japanese on its way to Java. He was picked up by another ship, which was in turn torpedoed and sunk by the Japanese (Bill Kesnick, 18 December 2017). Christensen had originally enlisted from Chicago, Illinois, in 1937. His citation in part reads:

> … *procured a rescue breathing apparatus and a fire hose, entered a cargo space strange to him and extinguished a fire when a bomb exploded in the compartment.*[43]

---

[43] Department of the Navy, Bureau of Naval Personnel. "Information Bulletin, Number 306," September 1942, 20.

Normandy:
A Father's Ship and a Son's Curiosity

Crew

Of the fifty-five crew members who boarded *PC 552* initially, only fourteen were present at D-Day. The rest of the crew members were replacements. Those fourteen crew members were as follows: Robert Geweniger, William Kesnick, Edward Lemme, Charles Penny, Conrad Schmidt, Ray Smith, William Steele, Edward Stefanek, Roland "Nick" Stine, Joseph Stone, George Sullivan, Lawrence Sullivan, Richard Van Wormer, and Thomas Williams.

Of those fourteen crew members, only five—Charles Penny, Conrad Schmidt, Ray Smith, William Steele, and George Sullivan—sailed the *PC 552* home in June 1945.

Of all the crew members who boarded the USS *PC 552* on 30 July 1942, only one stepped off the ship when she was decommissioned 18 April 1946: Boatswain's Mate Second Class (BM2c) George Clinton Sullivan, USN, who had boarded with the rate of able seaman (AS). The last plank owner, he had enlisted 05 May 1942 from New Haven, Connecticut.[44] Perhaps he took the plank with him.

Sailors have both a rate and a rating. The rate is a level of authority (such as first, second, or third class—what most would call rank), while a rating is a general occupation (such as a radioman). Only officers have rank.

The crew present could vary a lot. For example, the ship was often short of officers early in the war, so officers being transferred to other duty stations via the *PC 552* would serve as watch officers for the voyage but were not officially assigned to the ship. The same

---

[44] "Muster Roll of the Crew of the USS PC 552," the official ship's muster compiled each month by the yeoman and signed by the executive officer (XO).

occurred with enlisted men. In its last year, the ship had a skeleton crew, which would wax and wane based on a number of factors. In reality, a patrol craft was so small the relationships between the ranks was informal, unlike on major vessels, so duties were shared.

For a list of every sailor who officially served aboard the USS *PC 552*, see appendix A.

Commanding officers (CO)

The following is a list of the commanding officers:

Table 3. Commanding officers

Commanding Officer	Dates Served as CO	Days
Lt. Donald McVickar	29 Jul 1942–28 Nov 1942	122
Lt. J. Ross Pilling Jr.	28 Nov 1942–02 Oct 1943	308
Lt. (jg) Frank Pierce	02 Oct 1943–30 Sep 1944	364
Lt. A. Bradley Moll	30 Sep 1944–28 Jan 1945	120
Lt. James Spielman	28 Jan 1945–08 Apr 1946	435
Lt. (jg) Robert Gleason	08 April 1946–18 Apr 1946	10
Total (three years, nine months)		1,359
Source: Deck Log of the USS *PC 552*.		

For a list of commanding officers with more detail, see appendix B.

Other officers

PC 552 was allotted a commanding officer (CO), universally referred to as the skipper, an executive officer (XO), and two watch officers. Sometimes the watch officers had special duties, such as gunnery officer or communications officer, and sometimes they didn't. Patrol craft were informal. Many of the officers were promoted on the ship. For example, Lieutenant Moll came on board as the XO, rated LT. (jg); he was promoted to CO and Lt. Both Lt. (jg) T. F. Finucane and

Normandy:
A Father's Ship and a Son's Curiosity

Lt. (jg) W. J. Shaw originally came on board as ensigns and watch officers. Other officers were transferred to other ships.

For a list of other officers who served aboard the *PC 552*, see appendix C.

Individual medals

In addition to unit awards and individual medals earned for unusual efforts, most men of the *PC 522* probably received *all* the following medals:

Figure 38. World War II Victory Medal

The World War II Victory Medal was awarded to any member of the US military, including members of the armed forces of the government of the Philippine Islands, who served on active duty or as a reservist between 07 December 1941 and 31 December 1946.

Figure 39. European-African-Middle Eastern Campaign Medal

The European-African-Middle Eastern Campaign Medal recognized those military-service members who had performed military duty in the European Theater (including North Africa and the Middle East) during the years of the Second World War.

Figure 40. The American Campaign Medal

The American Campaign Medal recognized those military members who had performed military service in the American Theater of Operations during World War II. A similar medal, known as the American Defense Service Medal, was also awarded for active-duty service prior to the United States' entry into World War II. Some crew members received that medal also.

So what was needed to pave the way to D-Day?

7

Prelude to D-Day

The Americans worked hard to supply and transport the means of war to all the Allies. By themselves, they outproduced all the other countries combined and supplied the British, the Chinese, the Soviets, and others. As mentioned earlier, they stockpiled soldiers and munitions in southern England in anticipation of D-Day. After the assault, a former German soldier related how as a prisoner of war, he was transported down a road in England and saw huge stacks of crates on both sides of the road, all of which were stenciled with "Made in the United States." After the war, he decided to immigrate to this place called "United States," as he figured any country that could produce so much must be an amazing place with lots of opportunity.[45]

As soon as the Americans entered the war, the western Allies began to plan the assault on France to carry the war to Germany. A preliminary priority was to eliminate the Luftwaffe (German air force) to achieve air superiority over Europe prior to the invasion. This was a key objective of the long-range bombing runs over Germany and was the goal of Operation Pointblank.

Operation Pointblank

Operation Pointblank was as aggressive as it sounds. It was an eyeball-to-eyeball unrelenting raining of hell from the heavens over Germany. Operation Pointblank was devised to destroy Germany's means to produce and transport aircraft to achieve Allied dominance

---

[45] As related on the Quora forum, a personal remembrance. Soldier not identified.

of the skies prior to the invasion. It was a British-American effort, with the Americans focusing on bombing during the day and the British focusing on bombing during the night.

The American 8th Bomber Group bombed from England, while later the American 15th Bomber Group bombed from Italy after Italy had been invaded successfully. American bombers, aptly called Flying Fortresses, bristled with machine guns, the devil's pianos, and the airmen knew how to play them. Escort fighters were not capable of accompanying the American Flying Fortresses all the way to the targets, but the Allies believed the bombers would always get through because of their defensive weaponry. That turned out not to be the case.

Initial Allied fighter escorts returned to base after crossing the Channel, later to the German border, due to fuel limitations. After that, the bombers were on their own. Although the bombers were well armed, they were basically flying trucks without maneuverability. At the destination, bombing runs required a long, straight, predictable flight path, at which point the bombers were unusually vulnerable to attack. The flak guns flashed and roared, and the German fighters swarmed and shrieked around the bombers.

"The planes were not heated (temperatures reached 60 below zero *in* the plane) or pressurized so the crews had to fly 6 and 7 hour missions in heavy flight suits to keep warm and breath through oxygen masks. Day to day the crews based in England did not know what they might be doing the next day. They might fly missions on three consecutive days and then not again for a week or two. On a mission they could face up to three hours of flak guns and enemy fighters on their approach and then, under heavy fire, to maintain a steady straight course in the last leg to the target to ensure accuracy of bombing, followed by perhaps another three hours of combat as they flew back to England." "A Falling Of Fortresses: The Schweinfurt Raids," 14 October 2013. Blog: Things Have Changed. Accessed 29 August 2017.

Normandy:
A Father's Ship and a Son's Curiosity

The death toll began to seem inevitable. Day after day, hollow-eyed young men woke up in the cold, gray dawn to scrape the stubble off their faces, be fed and briefed, and climb into those massive planes—often with hands shaking from self-medicating the night before. On the flight across the Channel and France, the crew had time to reflect on the good chance they would not be returning from this mission and the statistical

Figure 41. B-17 G Flying Fortress "Wee-Willie"
This plane from the 322nd Bomber Squadron of USAAF 91st Bomber Group lost a wing from flak fire over Stendal, Germany, 08 Apr 1945. Eight were killed. You are looking at the last few minutes of their lives frozen in time. The pilot and one crewman survived. Germany surrendered one month later. Source: United States National Archives. 208-YE-142.

certainty they would not survive all of their missions. The planes lumbered through the air until they hit German airspace, at which point the American fighter escorts peeled off to go home and the German fighters came on relentlessly, the staccato of their machine guns flashing. Nonstop, the thirteen Flying Fortress machine guns chattered their songs of death, and the crew shouted to one another in warning for the next three hours while flak shook and rattled the planes. As the bombers flew through flak bursts, the unmistakable smell of cordite filled the cabins.

Finally, the planes settled in for the bombing run while the bombardier took over official control. The bombing run was one long, steady, predictable path, during which the crew expected to catch that fatal flak and begin the spiral downward any moment. When the bombs were released, the planes lurched up into the air from the reduction in weight and made a hard upward swerve to return home.

With luck, as the bomb bay doors shut, the planes raced for three hours to the border, fighting off German fighters the whole way. If they didn't go down in Germany or France, dive into the freezing Channel, or crash over England, they came home to

Figure 42. "Happy Day!! The End of My Combat Tour
Leiston, Eng. Aug. 16, '44. Harry." P-51 "Betsy."
We hope Harry made it home.

a meal and a shower, still feeling the vibrations in their hands and the planes' rumblings in their heads. Back in the Quonset huts, they sat on their bunks and resumed self-medication while noting the empty bunks that just that morning had held their comrades. They expected to be next.

The Allies took a lot of casualties, and the outlook began to look grim. This culminated in the 14 October 1943 bombing raid on Schweinfort, an important German center for the manufacture of ball bearings, deemed vital for aircraft manufacture. The 291 bombers took off with 2,910 crew members. Only 257 bombers made it to Germany, where they were without fighter escorts for the remainder of the three-hour trip to the target. Only 229 bombers made it to Schweinfort for the bombing run. Of the total bombers engaged, sixty were shot down and lost with all ten of their crew (six hundred men), and only 197 made it back to England. Of those, five were abandoned or crashed upon reaching England, and seventeen landed but were so damaged they were scrapped. Only ninety-three returned unscathed.

This was called "Black Thursday," but that October was bad in general. That fall of 1943, most bomber crews became very fatalistic and assumed they would not make it through the war.[46] The Allies cut back on bombing runs for a few months until this could be sorted out.

In answer, the Americans introduced the P-51 Mustang, the Flying Undertaker, a legendary fighter bomber escort. The Mustangs were able to escort the bombers all the way to the heart of Germany and take on the Luftwaffe while the bombers did their jobs. Several sources report that Hermann Goering, the head of the Luftwaffe, said, "The day I saw Mustangs over Berlin, I knew the jig was up."[47] Some squadrons of Mustangs accompanying the bombers were assigned to stay close to the

Figure 43. Comin' in on a Wing and a Prayer
What a show! What a fight!
Boys, we really hit our target for tonight
How we sing as we limp through the air
Look below, there's our field over there
With our one motor gone
We can still carry on
Comin' in on a wing and a prayer.
Number-one song on the pop chart in July 1943 by the Song Spinners.
Songwriters: Harold Adamson and Jimmy McHugh. Source: Wikipedia.

---

[46] Elmer Bendiner, *The Fall of Fortresses* (New York: Putnam, 1980). The author realized during the briefing for the second Schweinfurt raid that only four of the eighteen crews from the first raid were still around only two months later for the second raid. Six of the seventeen bombers from his squadron that took off that day for the second bombing raid failed to return. After that came a third raid.

[47] This quote is in so many books, magazines, and other literature that it is now impossible to determine the original source. The sentiment rings true, but I can't help but wonder whether there is really a German word for "jig" in this sense.

bombers to protect them, while other squadrons were instructed to peel off to take the German fighters head-on, their red-rimmed eyes glaring with rage.

For some, an attack inspires fear. For others, it inspires a deep sense of outrage, as if it is a personal insult directed only at you. A little button you didn't even know you had gets pushed in the back of your head. The blind anger gives you strength to overcome. It is only after it's over that your stomach becomes upset and your hands shake.

Operation Pointblank was almost a defeat for the Allies, but instead, it was a major victory, though not for the reasons assumed. German fighter production actually increased in spite of the bombing runs as the Germans dispersed manufacturing abilities underground. However, the relentless bombing attacks required the German fighters to relentlessly respond. More German fighters were chewed up in attacking the bombers than could be produced, and so the Allies did wind up achieving the goal of destroying the German air force—just not for the

Figure 44. Col. Jimmy Stewart receives the Croix de Guerre with Palm for exceptional services Stewart's first love was the US Navy Academy. When his father refused to allow him to attend, he switched to Princeton, where he discovered acting. He continued flying on the side, and when the war came, he joined the US Air Corps. He flew twenty combat missions with the 8th Air Force and retired in 1968 as a general. Although he handled it well, he suffered trauma. He channeled that trauma as he played George Bailey in *It's a Wonderful Life* and was nominated for an Oscar. The realistic anxiety and anger George Bailey exhibited was pent-up PTSD. Source: NARA.

reasons expected. We take the good when it comes, however it comes, without questioning it too closely.

The shift in air focus

While Operation Pointblank continued, bombers were diverted to destroy the French railway system around Caen to make it very difficult to deploy German troops where needed on invasion day. This occurred in accordance with the Transportation Plan of Operation Overlord, the invasion plan. Bombers were also diverted to attack local air force bases, including German fighter planes and airfields. Allied fighters began to strafe local airfields around the clock. Final heavy bombing occurred near the beaches the morning of the invasion prior to the soldiers' arrival, but it was less effective, particularly on Omaha Beach.

Omaha Beach

In fact, the biggest failure was the ineffectiveness of the bombing run on Omaha Beach before the attack, which was a result of certain strategic decisions and not the bombing crews' fault. The bombers over Omaha came in from the sea and over the beach with the goal of dropping their ordinance on the beach, then turning around while inland. They were instructed to err on the side of not dropping their ordinance on the invasion force—sound wisdom. Unfortunately, there was little visibility, so while erring on the side of caution, the bombers completely overshot their targets. A more effective approach would have been to come in from either flank of the beach and bomb parallel to the beach, as was done at Utah Beach. Of course, that would have been much more dangerous for the bombers. It is not for us to second-guess the decisions made under pressure almost a century ago from the safety of our couches; however, the American fighting men who charged Omaha faced relatively unscathed German fighting positions.

Overall, the air campaign was very successful. The Allies dominated the skies above Normandy on D-Day, and the western Allies continued to dominate the skies above Europe for the remainder of the war. The Luftwaffe launched only about a hundred sorties the afternoon of D-Day, mostly by single-engine aircraft. The remainder of the war, gallows humor making the rounds of the German troops was that if the planes overhead were silver, they were American; if they were blue, they were British; and if they were invisible, they were German.[48]

Diversion

The most logical place to attack France was Pas de Calais because it was only eighteen miles from England and had a major port. Unfortunately, the Germans had heavily defended it. Accordingly, the Allies ignored Pas de Calais and selected the beaches of Normandy to assault France. The Americans provided artificial docks called Mulberries, which were towed to the beaches after they were taken. Through most of June, these were used to supply the assault. Cherbourg, a major port, was captured by the end of June, and by then the Allies had all the benefits of Pas de Calais.

Deception

Prior to the invasion, the Allies engaged in activities to make the Axis think the attack was going to be on Pas de Calais through Operation Bodyguard. A fictitious First US Army

Figure 45. Ghost tanks
Members of the 23rd Headquarters Special Troops (the Ghost Army) move an inflatable tank. Source: NARA.

[48] Stephen E. Ambrose, *Citizen Soldiers* (New York: Simon & Schuster, 1997).

Group, created and headed by the real General Patton, centered on
southwest England, issuing endless realistic radio chatter. Inflatable
Sherman tanks, landing craft, and other weapons of war were
stationed all around the logical jump-off point for Pas de Calais. It
can be quite amusing to see an old film in which one soldier rolls
over a very realistic "Sherman tank" by himself. The Allies also
bombed around Pas de Calais to make it look like that was the real
goal and the night before D-Day sent swarms of aircraft to drop
aluminum chaff across the Channel along the route to Pas de Calais
to make it look to the German radar like an armada was coming. The
Allies did a lot more, too, including spy craft and even sending a
General Montgomery look-alike to North Africa, where the Germans
would see him. In the end, the diversion was successful, and
Normandy was taken by surprise. Vital German reinforcements
remained at Pas de Calais for a week after D-Day until they finally
realized Normandy was the real thing. Those reinforcements could
have made a difference.

One drawback was that as part of the deception, Allied ships were
shuffled back and forth from English port to English port that
spring, like an American football quarterback faking a handoff to a
halfback. This was done to keep the Germans guessing where the
attack would come from. Because of this constant shuffling, some of
the ships never had time to rehearse before D-Day, which caused
confusion when the time came.[49]

Airborne assaults

Before and during D-Day, airborne units were dropped within
France to capture major objectives such as bridges and deny the

---

[49] Douglas L. Roberts, *Patrol Craft Squadron One, D-Day and Beyond* (Newcastle, ME:
1991), 8.

enemy the ability to rush in reinforcements. Under Operation Tonga, the British (and Canadian) 6th Airborne Division was dropped to capture and hold bridges to Caen and to knock out artillery emplacements believed to be able to bombard Sword Beach. The States dropped the 82nd Airborne Division (All-American) and the 101st Airborne Division (either the Screaming Eagles or the Puking Buzzards, depending on whether you were a member).

Perhaps like most young men, these men were confident in their training, their equipment, and the certainty of their invulnerability. There were going to be casualties, but that always happens to the other guy.

The goal of these divisions was to help capture Cherbourg, help consolidate the landings, and take out gun emplacements. This included the famous 2nd Ranger Battalion, which scaled the cliffs at Pointe du Hoc to take out the gun emplacements there. These parachute drops occurred just after midnight on D-Day. They were followed by glider planes loaded with soldiers, who were towed to the objective, then released to glide

Figure 46. 101st Airborne
Private Clarence C. Ware of San Pedro, California, applies last-minute war paint to Private Charles R. Plaudo of Minneapolis, Minnesota, in England before D-Day. Both sport Mohawk haircuts. Ware made it home, but we don't know about Plaudo. Source: US National Archives, # 111-SC-193551. This became a style in the 101st Airborne. This inspiration is attributed to Sgt. Jake McNiece, part Choctaw. Source: NARA.

down to the target. These drops are controversial. The weather was bad, and the troops wound up scattered. Some objectives were achieved, but others weren't. In the end, we still have to believe having three divisions of infantry dropped behind the lines must have created a bad day for the Germans.

D-Day remains one of the greatest feats of planning, production, and logistics in history. As much was done as was possible to prepare the way for the Allied navy to make its way to the beaches of Normandy to discharge and support the invading army.

The *PC 552* played its part, and its crew did not expect to survive but did. It was time for the navy to facilitate the ground soldiers to do their part. Let's see how the *PC 552* got to D-Day from the beginning.

8
Deployments Prior to D-Day

1942

The *PC 552* was commissioned 29
July 1942 and deployed to the
Atlantic.

In the wider world

Elsewhere, in April of that year, the
Doolittle Raid bombed Tokyo. While
not of strategic value, it had
enormous symbolic value and caused
the Japanese to regroup. Fighting
went on in Papua New Guinea with
the Aussies and the Diggers (New
Zealanders). In May and June, the US
Navy repelled the Japanese at the

Figure 47. North Africa
Allied soldiers embark on
landing craft off the
Algerian coast in
November 1942. Source:
US Army.

Battle of the Coral Sea and the Battle of Midway, which ended
the Japanese offensive. Instead of a few years, the Japanese
Empire ran riot less than a year.

During the remainder of 1942, the United States began the
offensive against the Empire of Japan with amphibious landings
on Guadalcanal 07 August 1942. Japan responded with all its
might, as this was a test case, and Guadalcanal was not over until
09 February 1943. The British and the Germans began the Battle
of El Alamein in October, which resulted in a decisive British
victory. The Allies invaded North Africa in November with
Operation Torch and began the second front.

Normandy:
A Father's Ship and a Son's Curiosity

By August 1942, the US Navy had transformed from almost nothing in the Atlantic to an antisubmarine warfare presence so heavy the

> **US Naval Observatory Time Zones**
> Each time zone has been assigned a letter. Thus, the USS *PC 552* arrived in Florida on its way back from D-Day and set its time to Zone Q, known in the civilian world as Eastern Standard Time.

German U-boats retired from the American coast. The Americans aggressively attacked anything underwater that moved—and many things that didn't move. Radar and sonar were in their infancy, with nowhere near the clarity they have now, and it was considered better to be safe and attack indistinct shapes than to risk being sorry. Off Cape Hatteras, North Carolina, a.k.a. "Torpedo Junction," the Americans even unknowingly depth charged the Civil War ironclad USS *Monitor*, which sank in a storm eighty years earlier.

> **Military Time**
> All times are given as military time, the time the crew used. The military day has twenty-four consecutive hours, so 1:00 a.m. is 0100—not to be confused with 1:00 p.m., which is 1300.

Sources

The sources for the deployments and crew details are listed and described in the section entitled "Sources" at the end of this book. A particularly moving source is the "Ship's History," a three-page document written after the ship made it back home.

Reading the sources day by day and week by week, one can feel something of the spirit and soul of the times and men lingering in them. An observant person can feel the initial anxiety of deployment, the calming over time as the near Atlantic was mastered, the building excitement as the ship crossed the Atlantic to England, and the nervous anticipation and even resignation as they advanced on D-Day. These were real people who lived in real times, just as you live now in your times.

Deployments

The first entry in the deck log is 29 July 1942: "1410 hours: Lt Commander Sassley USN turned vessel over to Lt. Donald McVickar USNR as C.O. Ship was commissioned as USS *PC 552* and colors hoisted. The following were guests abroad during commissioning ceremonies: Captain Paul P. Blackburn USN (Ret), Mrs. J. R. Birmingham, Dr. Paive (?) W. Fuller, Mrs. William Carr, Mrs. E. Kennedy, Mrs. B. Campbell, Mrs. V. D. Cutting, Miss A. Cutting, Mr. F. C. Fisher, Mr. H. L. McVickar, Mrs. Donald McVickar, Mrs. H. C. Taylor, Miss C. Moss, Mr. Feunie (Finucane?), Mr. E. A. Stern." (The handwriting is difficult to decipher.)

The *PC 552* spent August loading ammunition and guns, cruising locally around New York, and going on a shakedown cruise to Boston. In September, crew members tested the ship's engines and communications, and the ship was assigned to the Eastern Sea Frontier, which was responsible for the coastal waters between Canada and Jacksonville, Florida. The ship plied the coastal waters between Tompkinsville, New York, and Guantanamo Bay, Cuba, on convoy duty.

Figure 48. Deck log of the *PC 552*
For 23 November 1942, in which a running encounter (six and a half hours) with a suspected German submarine is described. Source: NARA.

Nowadays, busy financiers walk and run past the former headquarters of the Eastern Sea Frontier without giving it a thought. It is located at 90 Church Street in the City of New

York and is known as the Federal Building. Then, the Federal Building was known as the USS *Concrete*.[50]

In the latter part of September, the ship made enemy contact twice and attacked twice, with inconclusive results, although crew members observed an oil slick. The ship was transferred to the Caribbean Sea Frontier, which was divided into three sectors: Panama, Trinidad, and Puerto Rico.

From time to time, ships reported finding signs of the enemy's work, such as floating wreckage; drifting lifeboats, some with survivors and some not; and lonely life preservers.

PC 552 made a minor attack against a suspected German submarine in October and a few big ones in November, including one that lasted six and a half hours, with the help of the HMS *Halifax* and airplanes—no proof of results.

Figure 49. Lieutenant Pilling on the *PC 552* He went on to be the XO of the USS *Gandy*. He attended MIT and eloped with Bettie Keen in 1932 (to whom he was married the rest of his life). They had one daughter, Sara Pilling, before the war started. He and Lt. Pierce remained lifelong friends, and the two used to run together most weekends at the Saddle and Cycle Club in Chicago. According to Sara Pilling, "This was one photo that *always* sat on my mother's bureau ('til she died in 1995). I believe that I remember that the parrot bit him on the ear!" Source: Sara Pilling.

---

[50] Douglas L. Roberts, *Rustbucket 7* (Newcastle, ME: Mill Pond Press, 1995), 15.

Shipfitter second class Robert B. Christensen was presented with a Silver Star and a Presidential Citation for work he did before being assigned to the *PC 552*. The ship attacked another suspected submarine in November, and Lieutenant McVickar was transferred and replaced by Lt. J. Ross Pilling as the new commander of the *PC 552*.

One more suspected submarine was attacked in December, and the ship spent Christmas in Guantanamo Bay, Cuba.

Presidential Unit Citation

The ship was awarded the Presidential Unit Citation (PUC), per the deck log entry of 11 November 1942. This was awarded to units of the US Armed Forces, and those of allied countries, for

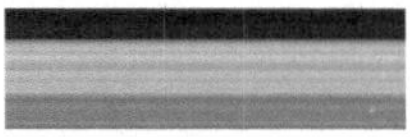

Figure 50. Presidential Unit Citation for *PC 552*

extraordinary heroism in action against an armed enemy on or after 07 December 1941 (the date of the attack on Pearl Harbor and the start of American involvement in World War II).

PC 552 should also have been awarded a Battle Star or Service Star for later efforts, but a record of such has not been located. Battle Stars were awarded for participation in battles, and the *PC 552* participated in two of them; Service Stars were awarded for campaigns.

Tompkinsville, New York

While the *PC 552* patrolled the Eastern Sea Frontier, Tompkinsville, New York, served as the ship's northern port. It is located on the northeast corner of Staten Island, across the water from and south of Brooklyn, where the ship was launched. During World War II, Tompkinsville served as the Navy Frontier base and included a major ASW training center, navy depot, and ship-repair center. Bill Kesnick learned radar there.

Guantanamo Bay, Cuba

Guantanamo Bay was the southern port. Guantanamo Bay, with an airport designation of GTMO (pronounced *Gitmo*), has served as a naval station for the United States since 1903. During World War II, it served as an intermediate distribution and consolidation center for convoys between New York and the Caribbean. It had a life long before the Afghanistan war.

A detailed summary of the deck log entries for 1942 is provided in appendix D.

> In reading the documents of that time, it seems the ships were always "degaussing." The Germans deployed a mine that detected the increase in the magnetic field caused by a large steel ship coming. Thus, the ship could be sunk without even hitting the mine. To counter this, periodically, the Allies wrapped huge cables around the ships and ran a current through them. This brought the ships' magnetic fields back to background levels.

1943

PC 552 performed protection for convoys going from New York (berthed at Tompkinsville) to Guantanamo Bay, Cuba, and back. For the most part, the navy performed serious maintenance, such as replacing guns, at Tompkinsville, which was also the main source for ammunition and new personnel.

In the wider world

The Japanese gave up Guadalcanal 07 February 1943. During the assault, the navy even considered the outcome in doubt at times and left the marines to finish the job alone without all their supplies. As a result, the marines were forced to live on captured supplies, trading shots in the rotting jungle, and urgently overrunning supply dumps. In commemoration, the marine officers struck an unofficial medal showing a navy arm dropping a hot potato into the arms of a marine with the motto *Faciat Georgius* ("Let George do it"). Ultimately, the navy came back, and the Guadalcanal campaign was successful. It broke the back of the Japanese defense, and the MacArthur island-hopping campaign began in earnest.

The Germans lost Stalingrad and Africa, Sicily was taken, and the Allies landed on Italy proper. Mussolini, the dictator of Italy, fell from power twice (reinstated once by the Germans). The marines landed on Makin and Tarawa Islands in the Pacific, and Dwight Eisenhower was named supreme allied commander.

Figure 51. "Sub Spotted"
Source: NARA, 513663.

Closer to home: the Tompkinsville spy

The ship's home yard remained the New York Naval Shipyard, and the ship's home base remained Tompkinsville, New York. Ironically, a German spy, Ernest Frederick Lehmitz, lived on Oxford Place at the top of the hill in Tompkinsville, where he could see the comings and goings of every convoy. He frequented the bars after work, drinking with sailors and getting what information he could. His neighbors thought he was above reproach, as he was dedicated to his victory garden and was an enthusiastic air-raid warden who never missed a blackout. He reported back to Nazi Germany through Spain in innocuous typed letters about his victory garden with the real messages written in invisible ink between the lines. He was not arrested until June 1943. He was given a prison sentence of thirty years as the result of a plea deal; he had been facing execution by the electric chair. He must have seen the *PC 552* come and go many times and perhaps had reported on it.

The deployments

The first half of the year was similar to how 1942 was: periodic contacts with potential enemy submarines, resulting in instant attacks by *PC 552*; great care given to zigzagging convoys; detailed deck log entries; and more.

These were anxious, serious men at an anxious, serious task. Under the tropic sun, the paint blistered and the crews baked. Their backs burned, and the skin peeled off of them. During the second half of the year, the convoys became routine. There were no contacts with potential enemies, there were less frequent convoys, and the deck log entries became cursory. Often, not even the name of the mooring station was mentioned. It apparently was not that important. On such days, the breezes sang their content in the halyards.

According to the deck log, *PC 552* attacked a potential enemy submarine in January, although the only evidence of success was the strong smell of fish oil. (Was this perhaps a joke about hitting a whale?) Convoys were routine in February and March.

> *For fifteen months she (PC 552) plowed the Atlantic and the Caribbean on this 'New York to Gtmo run' hunting for enemy subs and protecting the convoys entrusted to her unit. (Ship's History)*

In April, several important events occurred. The ship made suspected contact with an enemy submarine four times, three of them outside of New York. Each was vigorously attacked. Then there was another event important enough to make the deck log on 30 April 1943:

1405: Received aboard from Grimshaw's Confectionary, candy, soap + gum.

1503: Received aboard from Maritime Tobacco Co., cigarettes + book matches.

On 15 May 1943, the ship was credited with one submarine kill in concert with another patrol craft.

The remainder of the year was uneventful, and the *PC 552* was transferred back to the Eastern Sea Frontier in August 1943. The ship also received new guns and "plenty of ammunition" at Tompkinsville.

Figure 52. "They asked for it!"
"Yes, we believe that the Nazis and the Fascists have asked for it—and they are going to get it!"
Franklin D. Roosevelt, State of the Union Address. 07 Jan 1943.
Source: NARA.

In October, command was transferred from Lt. J. Ross Pilling to Lt. Frank Pierce. Lt. Pilling went on to be the XO of the USS *Gandy* (DE 764) destroyer, which destroyed another German submarine and captured members of its crew. His daughter recalled him in an email:

In the very few times that he [Lieutenant Pilling] talked of WWII, was his frustration and sense of despair watching merchant ships be torpedoed (and sunk) while performing escort duty—NY to

Normandy:
A Father's Ship and a Son's Curiosity

England…he…(also)…spoke of the fun times, especially strong relationships with the British Navy.

—Sara Pilling

In December 1943, the ship arrived from Guantanamo for the last time, as it had been selected to go to Europe. The ship was originally assigned to the Eighth Fleet (Mediterranean), then reassigned to the Twelfth Fleet (Europe).

The *PC 552* left Tompkinsville, Staten Island, New York, in the company of Destroyer Escorts (DE) *181*, *318*, and *225* and PCs *553* and *1225* to escort the convoy New York Section UGS 28 (**U**nited States to **G**ibraltar-**S**low) to Norfolk, Virginia. In late December, the ship went into dry dock at Portsmouth Navy Yard in New Hampshire to have its bottom scraped and painted in anticipation of the coming year.

Figure 53. "We've Just Begun to Fight!"
Source: NARA. Record Group 44. Records of the Office of Government Reports, 1932–1947.

"552" dropped her share of depth charges and rockets and received credit for a possible "kill" in company with another PC. (Ship's History)

I have included a detailed summary of the deck log entries for 1943 in appendix E.

1944 (to D-Day)

1944 was the year of the *PC 552*'s ultimate test.

In the wider world

Elsewhere in the world during the first half of 1944, the Battle of Anzio in Italy, which included a young soldier named Audie Murphy from Hunt County, Texas, began; the Allies began the massive bombing of Germany; and the Allies captured Rome.

Deployments

During this phase of the war, the *PC 552* protected a convoy across the Atlantic as the Western Allies built up the naval fleet in anticipation of the Normandy invasion. It then patrolled the European theater coasts and was based in Dartmouth, Devon, Plymouth, and Falmouth, Britain, and after D-Day, in Cherbourg, France. On D-Day, it served as one of the control vessels for Omaha Beach.

Figure 54. Dr. Seuss
Even Dr. Seuss got into the act. "How're we doing?" 09 May 1941, Dr. Seuss Political Cartoons. Source: Special Collection & Archives, UC San Diego Library.

Starting in December 1943, there was a renewed interest and urgency aboard *PC 552*. There was an immediate return to the emphasis of zigzagging convoys and meticulous entries to the deck log. Things were serious again. All seemed to know this was the beginning of the big show, with D-Day being the biggest part. It is clear from reading the ship's documents that the crew members knew D-Day was to be one of the deciding events of the war and that the transatlantic crossing was the prelude to that deciding event.

Figure 55. Crossing the Atlantic
The *PC 552* crossing in rough seas. Source: William Kesnick.

It was not over after D-Day. The Germans continued to strafe and lay mines the remainder of the year. The Germans still held the Channel Islands, which served as a military base from which to launch attacks. There still was a concern regarding enemy submarines.

It was Lieut. Pierce who brought the "552" into New York, on 17 December 1943 on what was to be her last trip from Guantanamo. For she had been selected as one of the multitude of vessels that was to play a part in the great land, sea, and air operations in northern France. (Ship's History)

Crossing the Atlantic

On 05 January 1944, the ship joined a bigger convoy designated UGS 29. As part of Task Force 69, the *PC 552* joined the *PC 1225*, *PC 553*, and several destroyer escorts to convoy UGS 29 across the Atlantic to the United Kingdom. Convoy UGS 29 consisted of fifty-three merchant ships; the army tug *LT* (Large Tug) *221*; the *LST*s (Landing Ship, Tank) *22, 8*, and *44*; the *LCI*s (Landing Craft, Infantry) *493–503*; and the carrier USS *Guadalcanal*, with escorts. All men knew this was the start of the big show.

The *PC 552* broke off from the main convoy approximately 527 miles southwest of Ponta Delgada, the Azores, as Task Force

69.2.[51] This task force included the *LCIs* (Landing Craft, Infantry) *493–503*, escorted by the *PCs 552, 553*, and *1225*, and headed to Horta, Fayel, the Azores. The ship's evaporator broke down, and the ship was with little fresh water. It was a very rough crossing. The ship remained at Horta because of intense weather.

Douglas L. Roberts, in his book *Patrol Craft Squadron Number One: D-Day and Beyond*, gave an account of his crossing in the *PC 617* later in March 1944:

> Oh, gather 'round me, comrades; and listen while I speak
> Of a war, a war, a war where hell is six feet deep.
> Along the shore, the cannons roar. Oh how can a soldier sleep?
> The going's slow on Anzio. And hell is six feet deep.
>
> Praise be to God for this captured sod that rich with blood does seep.
> With yours and mine, like butchered swine's; and hell is six feet deep.
> That death awaits there's no debate; no triumph will we reap.
> The crosses grow on Anzio, where hell is six feet deep.
>
> —Audie Murphy, 1948

Audie Murphy was a war hero, yes, but not many people realize he was also a gifted poet. Few people know he also constantly, although successfully, battled PTSD after the war.

Crossing the North Atlantic in wintertime was always a demanding task, but for the small escort craft it was real punishment. It was a twenty-six day crossing and the sun shone on only two days. The high seas caused tow lines to be parted. Barges cast loose in the heavy seas broke in two and had to be sunk by gunfire. Lives were lost when crewmen tried to retrieve broken tows.

---

[51] The source document actually lists "Task Force 62.9," but this appears to be a typo. Task Force 69.2 would be the second split-off of Task Force 69, the original task force.

Normandy:
A Father's Ship and a Son's Curiosity

There were many narrow escapes when crews were almost lost overboard from the small vessels in the heavy seas.

(Roberts, pp. 3–4)

Patrol craft were equipped with two massive diesel engines, which were really repurposed locomotive engines. They were designed for overwhelming, instant torque, which meant they could not gradually increase speed. The instant speed tended to break tow lines. Because of World War II, the United States continued with railroad steam engines longer than it would have otherwise, as the diesel engine production capacity was shifted to military craft.

Patrol craft were not designed for cross-ocean travel. They did not carry the fuel and supplies necessary to make it. One ship in the convoy was designated the convoy fleet oiler. A patrol craft had to be refueled in the middle of the ocean about every six days by this fleet oiler. If the fleet oiler caught a torpedo, it would be a disaster for all, as the patrol craft would be in the middle of the ocean without sufficient fuel to make it back to either coast. Protecting the merchant ships was very personal to the crew of the patrol craft.[52] The crew had its heart in its collective mouth the whole way. Periodically, sailors noted high-level German planes observing their progress, but that is all. The biggest enemy observed was the weather, but that was bad enough. In the North Atlantic, ice[53] covered the guns and the lines and had to be chipped away.

---

[52] Douglas L. Roberts, *Rustbucket 7* (Newcastle, ME: Mill Pond Press, 1995), 83.

[53] Anyone who has suffered frostbite will tell you it takes years to get completely over it. The formerly frostbitten skin becomes highly sensitive to

James F. Morgan also speaks of those times in his book, *History of USS Riverhead (PC 567)*. He was in the same convoy as the *PC 552* and wound up at Omaha Beach:

> *The next day conditions became worse with sea conditions reaching the scale of (Category) 5[54]...These were 60 foot seas. One huge breaker rolled over the entire ship, covering it with tons of foamy water causing it to take a roll of 60 degrees, first to port and then back to starboard. The convoy was scattered for miles around and radar was useless in such huge sweeping seas.[55]*

The most dangerous times were dawn or dusk. At those times, the vicinity of the ocean was too dark to note the sinister sight of a U-boat periscope popping up, readying a torpedo. At the same times, the ships were silhouetted against the beautiful majesty of the rising or setting sun, dark shapes against an orange sky. The U-boats could see the ships, but the ships could not see the U-boats. Many convoys went to General Quarters as a policy at dawn and dusk.

The convoy left Horta as part of Task Group 120.2, which included as additional escorts the *PC*s *552, 553,* and *1225*. Vessels escorted were the *LCI*s *493–502*. The convoy was bound for the Tamer River, Dartmouth, Devon, but was seriously delayed by the weather. There were several false alarms, but the convoy

---

breezes, and a light breeze most people would not even notice seems painfully cold.

[54] This was a hurricane. Scale 5 equals wind speeds of 249 km/h (155 mph) or more. (This is the highest scale.)

[55] James F. Morgan, *History of USS Riverhead (PC 567)* (St. Petersburg, FL: privately published, 1992), 24.

arrived without incident in time to experience the nightly Nazi air raids.[56]

This was their (crew and officers') first look at open warfare as they witnessed the German bombings of England's south coast. (Ship's History)

One member of the crew, Nick Stine, recounted in an interview (see chapter 11) his feeling when first encountering war directly:

"When we went ashore there, I was dumbfounded of the villages and little developments along the way," Stine said. "Hitler had already blown the hell out of all of them. As we went forward up to the other end (of the river) where they were, they were still blowing the hell out of anything in their way. War is just the damndest, lousy experience by the way it's born."

Stine's family said he once described it as a moonscape by the way the artillery (sic bombs) blew holes in the buildings and ground.

"Hitler had gone in and shot up everything in there—villages, homes, everything," Stine said. "We stayed

Figure 56. Rosie the Riveter fashion
The smart young women of the times sported the "Rosie the Riveter" look. This was a simple coverall, often with a bandana covering the hair. Women were encouraged to cut their hair short so as not to get it caught in machinery. Somehow, the men's overalls never looked this good.

---

[56] Douglas L. Roberts, *Patrol Craft Squadron One, D-Day and Beyond* (Newcastle, ME, 1991), 4.

through that and went to the north end. It was pretty much the same thing." [57]

While getting used to the nightly air raids, the sailors quickly found they could occupy their time by watching the various women on shore going about their lives. All available binoculars were instantly put in use, but the sailors quickly realized the best were the gunsights. Thus, a young woman might walk down the landing unaware of that ship in the distance training its weaponry on her.[58]

Sea legs and land legs

Getting our sea legs is a natural and necessary phenomenon. As we run down a gangway on a pitching and rolling ship, our bodies quickly and subconsciously learn to adjust so that what looks like an erratic run all over the gangway is really a straight line in space. We quickly get to the point where we can run down a rolling deck at top speed and not even notice the roll (after we get over our seasickness). We have gotten our sea legs.

With the first landfall, the opposite effect takes place. The legs unconsciously adjust for the roll and pitch of the ship, but the land is steady. The result is we feel we are rolling and pitching all over the place, even as our brain tells us we are on stable, dry land. The effect is bizarre and unsettling. It takes a while to get our land legs back. I am sure the crew of the *PC 552* experienced this when they reached England.

---

[57] Stephen Green, "Montgomery County veteran remembers Battle of Normandy," *The Courier of Montgomery County*, 05 June 2015.

[58] Douglas L. Roberts, *Rustbucket 7* (Newcastle, ME: Mill Pond Press, 1995), 89.

Normandy:
A Father's Ship and a Son's Curiosity

The spring

The spring was spent convoying shipping around the coast of the United Kingdom and doing practice runs for the forthcoming invasion. The chief question on everyone's mind was when the real action was going to happen. In March 1944, two soldiers were wounded from shrapnel during training and were attended in part by the pharmacist from the *PC 552*. One later died.

Falmouth, Dartmouth, Plymouth, and Torquay will ever remain in the minds of those who served aboard "552" during this period of preparation. As spring grew into summer, the tension became greater and officers and men were confident that the ship they had made ready and trained aboard would do her bit when the fateful day arrived. (Ship's History)

Figure 57. *LST-289* hit by U-boat
LST-289 was heavily damaged during Operation Tiger but made it back under its own power. Source: US Navy.

In April a practice invasion of Slapton Sands, England, called Operation Tiger was made. The *PC 552* was involved but experienced no incident; however, the convoy behind the *PC 552* was attacked by German E-boats, torpedo boats capable of 40 knots of speed, that snuck in during the night. The *PC 552* at the time noted only sporadic light against the sky from gunfire in the distance. The next day, crew members learned more than seven hundred Americans had been killed—more than those lost in the assault on Utah Beach on D-Day.

Nine German E-boats, like unleashed greyhounds, raced across the Channel, slipped past the outer patrols, and launched

93

torpedoes. Gunfire broke out, and all the Allied ships went to General Quarters. Three Landing Ship Tanks (LSTs) were torpedoed.[59] Two were sunk, and one was hurt but exchanged gunfire as it made its way to the beach. The E-boats deployed covering smoke and escaped at high speed.[60]

LSTs were massive flat-bottomed ships designed to be beached if necessary. In the bow were two large doors that opened to allow the tanks to drive directly onto the beach. They held about 20 tanks and about 250 men and were armed. The causes of the Slapton Sands incident were poor synchronization of radio frequencies, which resulted in no communication; lack of adequate escorts; and a life belt mistakenly thought to be designed to be worn around the waist but actually designed to be worn under the armpits. When the men jumped in the water, the force of entering the water slammed the life belt up the torso into the head, which was heavily weighed down by the helmet, often breaking the neck. The *PC 552* flew its flag at half-mast in respect.

The next day local civilians noticed the bodies and general carnage washing up on the beaches with the lapping waves but were threatened to remain silent. This incident was not disclosed until 1985.

The secretary of the navy, William Knox, a veteran of the Spanish-American War and a Rough Rider with Teddy Roosevelt,

---

[59] Douglas L. Roberts, *Patrol Craft Squadron One, D-Day and Beyond* (Newcastle, ME: 1991), 6.

[60] James F. Morgan, *History of USS Riverhead (PC 567)* (St. Petersburg, FL: privately published, 1992), 25.

also died on 28 April 1944. He had charged up San Juan Hill. He was honored simultaneously by the *PC 552*.

In late May, the *PC 552* collided with another ship in the fog during more exercises. The collision crumpled the ship's bow. The ship had to be repaired and was not released until 03 June. This ratcheted up the crew's anxiety, according to the Ship's History. The sailors' nerves became raw and frayed.

I have provided a detailed summary of the deck log entries for 1944 prior to D-Day in appendix F.

9
It Begins

Before we come back to our little ship, the *PC 552*, we look at where it fit in the grand scheme of D-Day. It took its assigned place in that new armada on the way to Normandy. The western Allies had prepared for that day, and that armada had come together. The entire operation of becoming lodged on the European continent, the far shore, was called Operation Overlord.

The beaches

Succeeding generations have forgotten there was more than one beach on D-Day. Utah Beach (United States), Omaha Beach (United States), Gold Beach (United Kingdom), Juno Beach (Canada), and Sword Beach (United Kingdom) are names that can never be forgotten by those who lived through those times or their families. The forces that landed at Utah Beach had the goal of capturing Cherbourg with its port, which became the new home port of the *PC 552* after D-Day. The forces landing on Sword Beach, with significant American support, drove on to Caen and took that city. By far, the hardest beach was Omaha, or as it became known afterward, "Bloody Omaha." Bloody Omaha was where the *PC 552* was stationed.

The armada crosses

The navy operations themselves were known as Operation Neptune, a subset of Operation Overlord. Toward the end of May 1944, military units began to be sealed. Army camps were sealed, the officers of navy ships received their copies of Operation Neptune and returned to their ships, and the ships were sealed. Personnel were not allowed to enter or leave military units. The men of the *PC 552* remained in their cramped, sweaty ship while the officers figured out the role of the ship and its crew. Operation Neptune was 1,100 pages long and impossible to assimilate in a few days, so the officers focused only on the role of the *PC 552* and its surroundings.

On 04 June 1944 at 0315, the great armada began to cross the Channel for the big event on 05 June 1944. The soldiers were in their tanks, and the infantry was crammed into the stuffy holds of the various troop ships. As they made their way for their rendezvous with fate, the skies clouded and darkened, the winds picked up, and the waves rose. General Eisenhower

Figure 58. Convoy of LC I (L) crossing the Channel on D-Day
Ships as far as the eye can see. Each craft towed a barrage balloon to protect against low-flying aircraft. Source: US Coast Guard Collection in the US National Archives.

determined the weather was adverse to a successful landing, and the seven thousand ships, with their cargo of fighting men and weapons of war, returned to England to await further orders. The last ship returned about noon on 05 June 1944.

The weather subsided, and during the early hours of that evening, with the cramped, exhausted men unrelieved and without sleep during that cold black night, the ships regrouped and began the crossing of the English Channel again.

Operation Neptune used the ships of eight navies and was divided into two task forces. The Eastern Task Force had the goal of managing and supporting the British and the Canadian landings. The Western Task Force (Task Force 122) supported the American beaches: Utah Beach and, of course, Bloody Omaha Beach. Details were delineated in Operation Plan No. 2–44, also known as Onwest Two. It consisted of the battleships *Arkansas*, *Nevada*, and *Texas*, eight cruisers, twenty-eight destroyers, and one monitor as well as the various landing and support craft. The flagship was the USS *Augusta* (CA-31), a cruiser. This was further broken up into Assault Force U for Utah Beach and Assault Force O (124) for Omaha Beach, the latter flagged by the USS *Ancon* (FF). The USS *Ancon* was a former ocean liner acquired by the US Navy and converted to a headquarters and communications ship. Assault Force O included multiple British ships as well as four French ships.

The beaches were divided into seventeen sectors, with Able (modern Alpha) to the far west on Utah Beach all the way to Roger (modern Romeo) to the far east on Sword Beach. Most sectors were further divided into Green, White, and Red. The sectors of Omaha Beach were Charlie (modern Charlie); Dog (modern Delta) Green, Dog White, and Dog Red; Easy (modern Echo) Green, Easy White, and Easy Red; and lastly Fox (modern Foxtrot) Green, Fox White, and Fox Red. The *PC 552* was assigned to Fox Green. These are just funny names to us now, but the men who participated in that landing weren't laughing.

Initially, the minesweepers came in and cleared a path for the
ships, marked by buoys. Mines continued to plague the Allies in
the weeks to follow, because the Germans sowed delayed-action
mines so that a ship could pass over them and not activate them
so that they weren't wasted on just a minesweeper. They might
detonate after several contacts, which would invariably be a more
valuable target, such as a ship full of soldiers. Two minesweepers
were lost to mines that day.[61]

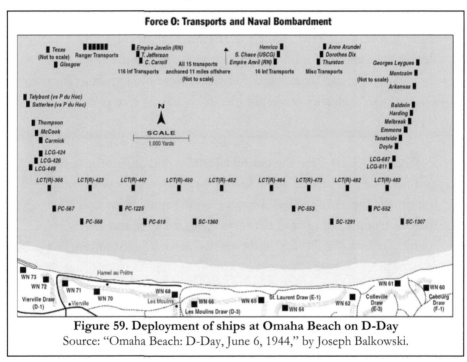

Figure 59. Deployment of ships at Omaha Beach on D-Day
Source: "Omaha Beach: D-Day, June 6, 1944," by Joseph Balkowski.

First to take their stations were the patrol craft, including the *PC
552*, leading the way and taking their positions closest to the
beaches before dawn. Some of the crew of the patrol craft racing

---

[61] Douglas L. Roberts, *Patrol Craft Squadron One, D-Day and Beyond* (Newcastle,
ME: 1991), 14.

ahead took the opportunity to "air" their bedding, draping mattresses over the life lines in an attempt to absorb incoming shell fragments.[62] Most of the crew had been assigned clothing and equipment to protect from gas attacks and wore them to the assault. Some patrol craft towed huge barrage balloons overhead to guard against air attack. They kept them for the next few weeks. To the *PC 552*'s immediate right flank were the *PC 553* and, farther away, the *PC 1225*, companions in the storm-tossed crossing of the Atlantic. Behind them were the Landing Craft, Tank-Rockets (LCT[R]), which were landing craft originally designed to land tanks but instead fitted out to launch 1,066 60 lb. rockets. Behind them, on either flank, were the Landing Craft, Guns (LCG), which were landing craft fitted out with two 25 lb. howitzers.

Behind the LCGs were the various destroyers that had the speed and flexibility to rush in and take out targets of opportunity when the time came. And behind them were the capital ships and various troop landing craft crammed with infantry and armor, many of which the *PC 552* had escorted across the Atlantic.

By the time the ships were in position on that cold, grim dawn, many men had been up for seventy-two hours and were exhausted, wet, seasick, and miserable.

The landing craft

All of us have seen photos of the Higgins boats (Landing Craft, Personnel and Vehicle, "LCPV") approaching Omaha Beach full of freezing, drenched, seasick infantry. We know the boats dropped their ramps and the men stormed their way through the

---

[62] Ibid., 16.

surf to the beaches, up to the bunkers, and beyond, even as some caught a round and crumpled to the ground.

In a later era, on a different continent, I disembarked from a ship by climbing down to a Higgins boat and assaulted a beach, so I write from experience. Ships disembark infantry soldiers for amphibious assault into Higgins boats by hanging huge rope nets over the side. The soldiers climb down these nets as they sway against the ships' hulls, encumbered by packs, weaponry, and general combat gear, and that rifle seems to get caught on *everything*. Imagine climbing down the side of a ten-story building. Sergeants rap the bone-white knuckles of soldiers who freeze at that great height and won't let go to climb down.

Great care has to be exercised near the bobbing Higgins boats, as they can rise and fall several feet on the ocean swells. A soldier has to time jumping off the net just right: too soon and the Higgins boat begins to drop as the soldier drops, resulting in a long fall with all that heavy equipment and screaming ankles and back; too late and the Higgins boat slams into the soldier when he's still on the net, leaving him tangled up in the net and confused, falling in a heap. If a soldier lands in the water, it may be all over, as that helmet can catch the water and break the soldier's neck, assuming he is not smashed between the bobbing ship and the landing craft.

When ready for D-Day, the Higgins boats regrouped, then headed to the beach with diesel engines roaring and the spray drenching the soldiers as the flat front ramp slammed into the waves. It turns out there is a reason ships have sharp bows, and that flat front ramp on a Higgins boat slams into each wave with a vengeance.

The secret to getting out of a Higgins boat in any order is to form up within the boat by rifle squad so the men can deploy to the left and right by cohesive squads ready for action. Otherwise, the men run out as a disorganized mob and take a while to form up.

What many people don't realize is that, for D-Day, the Higgins boats were used just for the initial waves. After the beaches were consolidated, the men came in Landing Craft, Infantry (LCI), which could be run upon the beach and lower gangways the soldiers could walk down on either side. The trick was to not be in that first wave of Higgins boats, though those who made it through Omaha Beach still had many obstacles ahead of them on the way to Berlin.

Figure 60. Disembarking from a Higgins boat on D-Day
Note bursts from the navy guns. Source: National Archives.

This was the same with tanks, which were carried forward by Landing Craft, Tanks (LCT). Behind them were LS(I) and LS(T), much bigger ships for the same purpose, which could also be beached and open huge bow doors to disgorge their contents.

The task of the first waves was to consolidate the beaches, neutralize the local fortifications, and take out the big guns. After this, the invasion at the beaches became almost an assembly line. As soldiers fiercely fought ahead to consolidate positions and advance, they were reinforced by new men landing on the beaches, walking down from the decks. They quickly moved forward to join the advance to be replaced by more men and equipment and ammunition and jeeps and artillery and other means of destruction, even as the shells continued to scream overhead and the wounded and dead were brought back. Eventually, temporary movable harbors called Mulberries were brought in, as well as artificial breakwaters. The unloading became like an industrial engine, feeding the raw, jagged front. This was not over by morning; it continued all day and the next day and the next day as the assembly line fed men and materials to their deaths or victory, as destiny allowed.

The beginning

Before dawn, the rocket craft, the gun boats, the destroyers, and the capital ships unleashed terror on Omaha Beach, and the Higgins boats and landing craft headed in, to be managed by the patrol craft. Principal among them was the Battleship *Texas* (BB 35), now a floating museum near Houston, Texas. Each ship had a predesignated target, and every ship participated, including the patrol craft, including Bill Kesnick and Ted Guzda on the aft 20 mms on *PC 552*.

As the morning sun rose over Normandy, the fire was shifted over the beaches to the hills beyond in an attempt to isolate the beaches from German reinforcements, provide suppressing fire,

103

and take out predetermined targets as well as targets of opportunity.[63] The Higgins boats approached Omaha Beach, diesel engines roaring and soldiers shivering and throwing up, with the 29th Infantry Division (the Blue and Gray) and some Rangers taking on the western half and the 1st Infantry Division (the Big Red One) taking on the eastern half. The shells mournfully wailed overhead.

Figure 61. Landing Craft, Infantry
USS *LCI 326* in England training for D-Day. Source: public domain.

Artillery can hold ground, but it can't take it; armor can take ground, but it can't hold it. Only the infantry, those lowly grunts, can take ground *and* hold it. In the end, it is always up to them. Those whom we colloquially referred to in the army as "(one

---

[63] A few years later, an infantry captain tasked with moving through a valley to Vierville related how he found a pillbox that would have stopped his company cold with much loss of life. Fortunately, he found the pillbox destroyed, and his company passed. *PC 567* had been assigned that pillbox. Morgan. p. 28.

each) nonelectrical pop up targets, olive drab in color" in a parody of the army nomenclature system.

Mulberries, Gooseberries, Corncobs, and Phoenixes

The Allies brought artificial, mobile ports called Mulberries, two six-mile-long steel piers that floated on the tide. Breakwaters were made with huge concrete-filled caissons called Phoenixes as well as old ships sunk in place called Corncobs. A row of Corncobs was called a Gooseberry. The Corncobs arrived about noon the day after D-Day. They were lined up, and huge explosions rocked the sea as they were sunk in place one after another. All this was as planned and explained in Operation Neptune, but the ships' crews had not had time to understand the complete plan and instead focused only on studying their tasks. They didn't know about the Corncobs. Much to their shock and horror, the men on the patrol craft saw Allied ships sunk one after another. They thought some sort of new German artillery with ungodly accuracy was being unleashed on the ships and it was only a matter of time before they would be taken out by the same means. They were mightily relieved to learn the truth.[64]

Patrol craft on D-Day

Of special note on that day, *PC 484* helped sort the landing craft on Utah Beach. Omaha Beach was so heavily defended the underwater demolition teams had not blown up all the obstacles. This caused a traffic jam of landing craft well into the afternoon. *PC 617* and *PC 618* had to keep the landing craft for Omaha Beach in order, even as they received machine gun and German

---

[64] Douglas L. Roberts, *Patrol Craft Squadron One, D-Day and Beyond* (Newcastle, ME: 1991).

88 fire. *PC 553*, *PC 567*, and *PC 568* raced into the shallow waters to directly confront enemy fortifications.[65]

The job of the *PC 552* was to control the landing of the 741st Tank Battalion, then successive infantry waves, all the while providing suppressing fire, rescuing fallen soldiers, and dodging German 88 artillery. And now we come to its story.

---

[65] Ibid.

10

D-Day and June

In the wider world

Rome fell on 04 June 1944—this was a big deal, but it was hugely overshadowed by D-Day on 06 June.

The beginning

On 04 Jun 1944, the *PC 552* took on all supplies and arrived at Poole Bay to be berthed alongside *PC 553*. *PC 552* received Operation Overlord (battle plans for the invasion of Normandy) from the USS *Samuel Chase*, and the crew took immediate action to understand, in the limited time available, the battle plan. *PC 552* proceeded to her assigned station in Poole Bay and anchored at 2209.

From: Naval Commander, Western Task Force

To: ALL HANDS

Subject: Coming Events

"In this force there are battleships, cruisers, and destroyers. There are hundreds of landing ships and craft, scores of patrol and escort vessels, dozens of special assault craft. Every man in every ship has his job. And these tens

Figure 62. Crossing on D-Day
USS *PC 552* in rough seas. This picture was taken on D-Day. It shows how rough the seas were. Note the whitecaps. Source: William Kesnick.

of thousands of men and jobs add up to one task only—to land and support and supply and reinforce the finest Army ever sent to battle by the United States. In that task we shall not fail. I await with confidence the further proof, in this the greatest battle of them all, that American sailors are seamen and fighting men second to none…

"Captains will please publish this letter at quarters on the day that ships are sealed; then post on bulletin boards; and remove and <u>burn prior to sailing</u>." (These final words were underlined by hand on the document.)

—Courtesy of William ("Bill") Kesnick

It begins

On 05 June, the ships were kept in the dark about the invasion's actual timing.

> *The secrecy surrounding the whole thing was uncanny. (Ship's History)*

As the ships began to congregate, the crew did not know whether this was the real thing or another rehearsal. As the number of ships increased, it soon became obvious. *PC 552* began rounding up its task force at 0222B and was underway by 0320B.

Figure 63. Deck log for D-Day
PC 552's deck log for D-Day speaks of heroism and death. Source: NARA.

The task force rendezvoused with the main assault group at 0930B. The weather was very rough, and several ships had trouble keeping station. USS *LCT (A) 2043* reported its engine room flooding and was in serious difficulty. *PC 552* passed over her only emergency portable pump, and the ship was able to continue. At

2225B, the *PC 552* received an SOS from the USS *LCT (A) 2229*. The ship was taking on moderate seas and was unable to jettison its cargo of tanks. *PC 552* took on the army personnel, and the ship was able to survive by leaving station. The convoy proceeded on.

Figure 64. Americans retrieve their dead on D-Day
Source: NARA.

It was not until several months later that the men talked of their humble feelings on that day when they learned that the time for invasion had actually come. (Ship's History)

On the morning of 06 June, *PC 552* arrived in the transport area off the coast of France at 0300B. The ship came to General Quarters at 0332.

At 0340, PC 552 synchronized watches with the USS Samuel Chase, then proceeded to her assigned station 4,000 yards from the beach at 0409B. As PC 552 left the USS Samuel Chase, Samuel Chase said over the loud hailer, "Good luck PC 552. Take your station." (Ship's History)

The ship, known as "*Rustbucket 552*" on the radio circuits, proceeded down the

Figure 65. D-Day casualties
A soldier from the First US Infantry Division stares at the camera as he is surrounded by injured comrades near Omaha Beach on 06 June 1944. He has been identified as Nicholas Fina, who lived in Brooklyn, New York. Source: NARA.

channel, which had been swept of mines and marked by buoys, then traveled to her designated line of departure at 0459B. The *PC 552* buoyed her line of departure for Fox Green Beach, then took up station as the Fox Green Beach patrol control craft.

As a patrol control craft, *PC 552* guided and controlled the invasion of Fox Green sector of Omaha Beach in Normandy. There were eighteen patrol craft in total at Normandy organized as PC Squadron One. During the Battle of Normandy, all PCs were under intense 50-caliber and artillery fire. *PC 1261* was sunk with significant loss of life by a direct hit by 88 artillery after being bracketed.[66] *PC 1176* had to take over for the *PC 1261*, as well as manage its original task.

Seeing God through a machine gun sight

Automatic weapons often include a tracer round as every fourth round. Tracer rounds show as a brilliant fluorescent light streaking across the sky, coming in bright colors of green, red, or gold—beautiful but deadly. The tracer rounds help the gunner aim his weapon by showing where the tracer rounds are landing. Automatic weapons are aimed as a garden hose is aimed.

A gunner will swear that the tracer light is a continuous line in the sky solid enough to walk on. The awe comes from realizing that what looks like a solid line is a series of discrete tracer rounds. The real awe comes from realizing that between each one of those discrete tracer rounds, there are three more rounds.

Barrels have to be replaced every few minutes or they become cherry red and start drooping. Asbestos gloves are issued to handle them. A

---

[66] This is controversial. Some early accounts claim the *PC 1261* was sunk by a mine. The men were just as dead either way.

barrel will become hot quickly, even if does not look like it. You will test this with your bare hand only once; you will never do this again.

Bracketing

When artillery and mortars are fired, the forward observers directing the fire must know both the range and direction. Direction is fairly easy to determine using a compass adjusted for the grid-magnetic difference, but range has to be estimated. The forward observer (pre-GPS) estimated a range and watched where the round landed. If the round landed short of the target, the difference was estimated again, and the observer directed the artillery to fire at what was estimated to be double the short fall. This continued until the round landed over the target. At such point, the target was deemed "bracketed." The next order was to direct Fire for

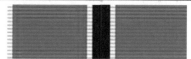

Figure 66. Bronze Star
Earned by Lt. Frank E. Pierce, junior, DV(S), the skipper of the *PC 552* on D-Day.

"For meritorious service in active sustained operations against the enemy in the Bay of Seine, France, for various periods of time in the Area Screen of the Naval Western Task Force, while participating in the invasion of France, June 1944."

Source: Frank E. Pierce III, the honoree's son.

Effect between the short fall and the over fall. Once a target was bracketed, it was a short period of time before it was obliterated, unless it moved immediately. When a person or ship was bracketed, it was immediately obvious, as was the need to shift position.

The first wave

At 0542, the first wave of attackers approached. The 741st Tank Battalion DD (duplex drive—both tracks for land and propellers for sea) Sherman amphibious tanks destined for the eastern half of Omaha, carried by *LCC-20*, were dispatched into the sea. At 0641, *PC 552* reported back to the USS *Chase*, "Entire first wave foundered." Unfortunately, on D-Day, the waves were too high, and many DDs destined for Omaha were swamped and sank while still well offshore. On other beaches, the commanders realized the danger and brought their DDs much closer inshore before launching, allowing more of them to reach the shore. The *PC 552* spent the next forty-five minutes (per the official account—some accounts say much longer) picking up survivors. The crew watched many of the soldiers drown in front of them, helpless to do anything.

> *On this historic day, all hands experienced for the first time, the terrible din of constant gunfire from shore, seaward, and from the air. (Ship's History)*

The *PC 552* became the focus of enemy artillery fire and was bracketed and within moments of being hit directly. An American destroyer from the gunfire-support group reduced the enemy installation before it could fire for effect. *PC 552* continued picking up drowning men while under heavy enemy fire. Seven men were rescued; another was picked up but found dead, and another was transferred to *PA 45-25*.

> *Some of those taken from the sea brought death aboard the ship for the first time. (Ship's History)*

Some soldiers were so weak from exposure that sailors from the *PC 552* had to be lowered by line to the water to place lines around the soldiers to pull them aboard. Those soldiers did not have the

Figure 67. Aerial attack on D-Day
Source: NARA.

strength to raise their arms to grab hold of the lines. Others were thrown life preservers attached to lines from the ship and were told to hang on (per Nick Stine).

That afternoon, *PC 552*'s SCR-609 radio quit working, so there was no communication with the beachmaster on Fox Green beach, which was under heavy mortar and small-arms fire. Accordingly, the ship was relieved of control duties at 1758B and commenced screening operations.

At the close of D-Day, 1740B, *PC 552*, along with the rest of PC Squadron One, was assigned to patrol the "Dixie Line," a ring of ships to protect the capital ships and transports from submarines and E-boats.

The German naval base at Cherbourg was still operational, and German Schnellboots (E-boats) attempted to infiltrate the Allied ships to attack them that night, only to find the ships amply defended by the patrol craft and the destroyers.[67]

The next morning, the remaining gliders full of soldiers were towed across the Channel and the beaches to continue the airborne assault. This time, the Germans were fully alert, and the crew watched as many of the slow-moving gliders full of soldiers were sent to their fiery deaths by the German 88s. It was, to use the language of the day, a turkey shoot.[68]

As the soldiers advanced over the hills, the sailors could no longer see the fighting except for periodic puffs of smoke in the distance. However, the sailors were reminded of the battle by the debris floating back to them with the tide: smashed equipment and supplies

---

[67] Douglas L. Roberts, *Patrol Craft Squadron One, D-Day and Beyond* (Newcastle, ME: 1991), 24.

[68] Ibid., 26.

and bodies and off in the distance, landing craft burning like funeral pyres, which they probably were.

The 741st armor-deployment disaster

Armor and infantry are best deployed together in the attack. Tanks can punch a hole through an enemy line with their speed, momentum, armor, and suppressing firepower to protect the infantry, but they lack visibility and the ability to hide. Unfortunately, they are also vulnerable to a lone soldier attacking from the lesser-armored rear or sides.

One tactic taught to infantry is to hide in a spider hole until the tank's flank is exposed, then run up to the tank with a log to jam between the wheels to force it to pop a track. An immobile tank is a soon-dead tank. The preferred method for this was what was then known as a bazooka, a portable tank killer. The purpose of friendly infantry in such an attack is to screen the flanks and rear of the tanks to protect them from these tactics and consolidate and hold ground taken.

The original plan called for the tanks to land first and protect the infantry while it landed; then the two could advance together. Unfortunately, most of the 741st foundered in the water, leaving the soldiers on Omaha to take the beachhead alone. The tanks were fitted with a canvas-and-rubber wall around the hatch to keep the water out. The tanks swam almost entirely underwater with a foot of free canvas. They were seaworthy in a calm sea but unstable in a rough one. According to Bill Kesnick, the crew of the *PC 552* knew the seas were too rough for the tanks to survive, but orders were orders.

Normandy:
A Father's Ship and a Son's Curiosity

The 741st was assigned to Omaha Beach, and the 743rd Tank Battalion was assigned to Utah Beach. Both battalions were equipped and trained identically. In the event of a calm sea, the tanks were to be launched thousands of yards from the shore to swim in. If the sea was rough, the landing craft were to sail right up to the beach and release the tanks directly on land. The commanders of Utah Beach decided to do the latter, but inexplicably, the commanders of Omaha Beach decided on the former approach. Twenty-seven of the twenty-nine tanks of the 741st sank, while most of the 743rd made it, though they also incurred serious losses.

Many present at the time remembered those men struggling and dying in the water for the rest of their lives. It haunted them in their last days.

I have included below a report from Lieutenant Pierce about the tank-deployment disaster:

"From: Commanding Officer USS *PC 552*. (OMAHA BEACH)

At approximately this same time the sixteen DD tanks forming the first wave for Fox Green Beach were seen approaching the line of departure after having been launched from the LCTs *549, 602, 592, & 601*—3000 yards to seaward of the line of departure. At 0533B the signal for dispatching the first wave was hoisted and executed at 0535B, however it was noted that the DD

Figure 68. 741st Tank Battalion coat of arms

tanks were maneuvering with great difficulty and in the area of the line of departure first one and then finally all of the DD tanks were seen to founder. It appeared as though the canvas frame work around the top of the tanks buckled due to wave action and by the time the tanks had reached the area of the line of departure so much water had been taken aboard that buoyancy was lost. The entire area 200 yards to shoreward and 300 yards to seaward was filled with survivors, some in inflated life rafts, others with life jackets only. At this time the wind was from the west force 3, with a short choppy sea dad (sic) with a current setting easterly at about 2 knots. At 0542B the ship was maneuvered into various positions to try to pick up those survivors who had been unable to get into life rafts and (sic) between 0542B and 0620."

Figure 69. Sunken tank off of Omaha Beach
Source: Nicolas Job, underwater photographer.
http://www.nicolasjob.net. A MC4 & LCL production.

PC 552 raced to pick up survivors. Some required prolonged artificial respiration.

The sailors of the *PC 552* did what they could to rescue the drowning tankers, all the while under intense fire. Lieutenant Moll (XO of the *PC 552*) cited individual works of note as follows:

Table 4. Cited on D-Day

For the manner in which they went over the ship's side to assist men in being removed from the sea:
Vendetti, Patrick, MoMM3c Dooley, Arthur David, RdM3c Sullivan, Lawrence Ferrel, CBM(AA) Watts, Richard Albert, MoMM2c

Johnson, Kiernan Patrick, S2c
For their attention and assistance in caring for the men brought aboard:
Dooley, Arthur David, RdM3c
Robinson, Raymond Leo, SoM1c
Sheppard, Glen Calvin, SoM1c
Williams, Thomas Jefferson, SC1c
Woolever, Francis John, SK2c
For taking charge of men and directing first aid as needed:
Hill, William Robert, PhM1c

Lieutenant Moll summarized the men pulled from the sea as follows:

Table 5. Pulled from the sea

Men picked up alive:					
Clements, Harold R.	T-4	741 Tank Battalion	Hulsey, Woodrow	T-5	741 Tank Battalion
Henkelman, Leonard	Sgt.	741 Tank Battalion	Melanson, Gerard	T-5	741 Tank Battalion
McGowan, John R.	PFC	741 Tank Battalion	Metzger, Donald R.	PFC	741 Tank Battalion
Johnson, Herman R.	Cpl.	741 Tank Battalion	Hutton, Gale	Pvt.	741 Tank Battalion
Covington, John H.	2nd Lt.	741 Tank Battalion	Linguina, Vincent	1st Lt.	741 Tank Battalion
Caccavoni, Frank J.	PFC	741 Tank Battalion	Norwood, Clayton	Cpl.	741 Tank Battalion
Crisler, Norman	Sgt.	741 Tank Battalion			
Men picked up dead:					
Domenighini, Elmo	Unk	Unk	Belcher, D.	Pjx.	SMN GEGC
Transferred from the *PA 45-25*:					
Slodkowski, Walter	Cpl.	741 Tank Battalion	Greenside, Norman J.	Cpl.	741 Tank Battalion

This information comes from the deck log, but there may have been more picked up than this. Some may even have died after rescue. Preliminary death reports had a tendency to grow as more information was received.

"Bloody Omaha"

Over thirty-four thousand troops landed on Omaha Beach, and within an hour, the water of the beach was red with blood.

Normandy had been a sleepy backwater for the Germans. When German General Rommel inspected France that spring, he immediately began a massive fortification buildup. On Omaha Beach, the soldiers had to cross more than a thousand feet of open sand, then cross a minefield and cut through crisscrossing barbed wire. In comparison to the other D-Day landing beaches, the ground is dramatically steeper, with only four natural channels leading off the beach. Massive 150-foot bluffs overlook the beaches, and the Germans had some eighty-five machine-gun nests and thirty-five concrete pillboxes protected by land mines. Many of the machine guns were the dreaded MG-42, capable of firing 1,200 rounds per minute with minor heating of the barrel. The German also had enormous numbers of antitank weapons and artillery.

With all this, it is amazing *anyone* made it off the beach. Omaha Beach had the lion's share of ground casualties that day and was soon referred to as "Bloody Omaha." A random sample of Omaha Beach sand taken as recently as 2012 showed that 4 percent of the sand consists of small bits of shrapnel and the results of high explosions.[69] One wonders where the organic material comes from. The beach still remembers.

The Great Gale

The last of the artificial ports was finished 17 June 1944 and was fully operational, but on 19 June 1944, disaster struck. The worst storm in

---

[69] Wynne Parry, "Fragments of D-Day Battle Found in Omaha Beach Sand," *Live Science*, 05 June 2012.

forty years blew directly into the Bay of the Seine with winds approaching 70 miles per hour,[70] a category-four storm known as the Great Gale. As the wind shrieked and the rain lashed men's faces, ships smashed against one another, and the American Mulberry was completely destroyed. The storm continued unabated until 19 June 1944.

British war correspondent W. F. Hartin gave his personal account of riding out the Great Gale:

> *Suddenly, three times in succession, we were nearly capsized. As every man clung to the nearest hand-hold, the water hissed along the deck, burying the starboard half in boiling foam. We looked at each other without attempting to speak, because the same thought was in all our minds—"This is the end. She is not going to right herself." Each time the vessel swung back crazily to port it was if she were bracing herself for the final plunge, when she would roll over completely to starboard…The story of the next 12 hours is one of relentless fight, zig-zagging across these seas, when each turn might have been fatal.*[71]

Supplying the beachhead continued. The British were slowed down, but the Americans made a conscious decision to run their great ships right up on the beach where they could be unloaded with speed, knowing this would destroy the ships. Progress never slowed down. Actually, with the beaching of the ships, American progress increased.

---

[70] Martin Cherrett, "The 'Great Gale' wrecks the Mulberry Harbors," *World War II Today*. Accessed 09 September 2017. www.ww2.com.

[71] W. F. Hartin, "I Was There! - A Gale Nearly Wrecked Our Invasion Fleet," *The War Illustrated*, 21 July 1944: 53–54.

The *PC 552* lost its anchor just before the Great Gale hit. The anchor fouled on what Bill Kesnick was informed was an underwater cable. The crew pulled up as much of the chain as possible to save what it could, then cut it. The *PC 552* was forced to ride out the Great Gale before the wind, then after the Great Gale, replaced the anchor by cannibalizing a beached craft. Bill Kesnick was part of the landing party, and he explored a German pillbox.

Cherbourg

The ship suffered several bomb attacks by German planes over the next two weeks, including a very close miss of the stern. The next big push was for the port of Cherbourg, as the Bay of the Seine offered little protection from the violent Channel storms. The ships remained on station in close quarters for weeks in those storm-infested waters as there was no port for them nearby.

The patrol craft were engaged in the effort to take Cherbourg—escorting soldiers and supplies, patrolling, and looking for and destroying mines, the big danger. The patrol craft found and destroyed 133 mines.[72]

The 82nd and 101st Airborne Divisions had originally secured the approaches to Cherbourg on D-Day and shortly thereafter. The American 4th Infantry Division (Ivy Division) made the amphibious assault on Utah beach, consolidated it, and was joined by the American 9th Infantry Division (the Old Reliables) and the American 79th Infantry Division (the Cross of Lorraine, or the Lost Lieutenants). Together, with the help of a British commando team, they pushed forward to Cherbourg and took it 29 June 1944. The Germans completely destroyed the port facilities before retreating,

---

[72] Douglas L. Roberts, *Patrol Craft Squadron One, D-Day and Beyond* (Newcastle, ME: 1991), 32.

but the Americans, after clearing the mines and rebuilding the port, were open for business the second week of July. The patrol craft moved in 12 July 1944,[73] and the *PC 552* returned from repairs in Dartmouth to Cherbourg for the first time on 26 July 1944.

From then, the patrol craft escorted French fishing vessels full of potatoes to feed the hungry in Roen and other French cities.

On 28 June 1944, the ship recovered the body of Thomas M. Stamm, US Navy, and proceeded to Easy White Beach for burial.

For the next few months after D-Day, the ships continued to find bodies floating in the stormy Channel. After many weeks at sea, especially after the Great Gale, they were a difficult sight. The ships tried to identify the bodies. If they were not too bad, they were taken to France for burial. If they were too far gone, they were buried at sea, usually with a heavy mousetrap rocket to weigh them down, where they rest to this day.

I have included a list of the ship's crew present on D-Day in appendix G.

Now let the men speak for themselves.

---

[73] Ibid.

11

Personal Experiences

As of this writing (2018), I know of only one survivor of the *PC 552*, Bill Kesnick. Looking back, it is natural to feel the men and women who participated in World War II were stock characters in a great drama. It is easy to look at the events of those years and feel the outcome of World War II was foreordained. But it certainly did not seem that way to those involved at the time. They were often young men away from their neighborhoods for the first time, in an environment full of rumors and lacking solid information. At home, their families waited and hoped for the best, though they had little information on what was really going on with their loved ones, because the mail was censored. The events were very real, always in doubt, and with no assurance of success or even survival.

These events are long past now. Often, I noted a crew member's name, looked up the hometown, and used the many modern search technologies available to look for families who could be related. I sent out exploratory e-mails, and I was sometimes successful. I also searched for obituaries. I corresponded with survivors, as well as with many extended family members of both the survivors and those who have left us. Initially, some family members seemed confused when I brought up a relative who had been gone for decades and who was not often thought of now. Sometimes the confusion came across as suspicion. Slowly, the conversation would evolve over weeks and months as we compared their vaguely remembered family lore to the records and developed what was likely the true story. In time, the confusion would evolve to gratitude and appreciation as long-dead fathers and grandfathers were brought back to life, even if just for a moment. They became central to their families once again, and their exploits were celebrated and remembered on Christmas. They are now routinely mentioned on Facebook, a medium they likely could not have imagined in their lifetimes.

We received correspondence from all over the United States and as far away as France. Bill Kesnick touchingly sent my family a Christmas card in 2016 and 2017. We hope to receive one in 2018.

David Raup received the research of his father's World War II experience in time to have it mentioned at Sam Raup's eulogy. Neither Sam nor David had known the ship had come close to being sunk on D-Day—Sam Raup was a machinist's mate deep in the bowels of the ship, focused on keeping the ship running, and so was unaware of what was going on topside.

It was touching to receive original, unique documents in the mail from family members. To be trusted with such documents was an honor. The reasoning was always the same: they just wanted these people remembered.

One woman said she started each day by looking at her father's name, which I had posted on the Internet. Each morning, she pulled up his name on the Internet and said "hello" with memories of love.

Some crew members' children had known one another during the War but lost touch afterward. Through the efforts of this book, they were reunited. A lot of unintended but positive things came from this book.

As we read the following thoughts, we remember these were young and inexperienced men away from home for the first time; their experiences were real, and their fortunes were uncertain.

Normandy:
A Father's Ship and a Son's Curiosity

Bill Kesnick and Ted Guzda

Bill Kesnick and Ted Guzda were childhood friends and remained close buddies all their lives. They grew up together in Waterford, a neighborhood in Stamford, Connecticut, and finagled to be on the same ship together. They wanted to "get those sons of bitches who bombed Pearl Harbor."[74] When Pearl Harbor occurred, Ted walked the railroad tracks to New Rochelle, New York, to join the navy, a distance of about twenty miles. He was accompanied by his brother Matthew, who wanted to join the marines. When they arrived in New Rochelle, there was only a marine recruiting station, so Ted walked back home, then along those railroad tracks to New Haven (about forty miles), and found a way to join the navy.

Bill joined the navy a little later and was assigned to the *PC 552*. The two met again in New York, and Bill convinced Ted to serve on the *PC 552* with him. After the ship went to sea, it was determined Ted had joined

Figure 70. Ted Guzda and Bill Kesnick
Onboard USS *PC 552* next to their 20 mm Oerlikon on the port side. Source: Bill Kesnick.

the *PC 552* without authorization. Instead of being arrested for

---

[74] Angela Carella, "'They Have the Same Angel.' Buddies Reflect on Surviving D-Day," *The Stamford Advocate*, 06 June 2005.

desertion, as a punishment, he was permanently assigned to the *PC 552.*

On the way across the Atlantic to England, prior to D-Day, Ted received word that Matthew had been killed on Guadalcanal. Ted never found out where, or even if, his brother was buried.

When the Channel crossing began for D-Day, there were so many ships that Ted and Bill were not sure which were which. Neither expected to return alive from D-Day, and they felt their leaders did not expect them to do so either. When D-Day commenced, they soon were too busy to care.

Bill Kesnick and Ted Guzda together (as always) related their story in an interview published in two different newspapers, one of them *The Stamford Advocate,* published 06 June 2005:

> *The sea was still rough...Bill [Kesnick] lost his helmet while enemy planes were shooting and shore batteries were firing. We were back to back on 20 mm guns. I emptied a bucket of sand and told him to put it on his head and all you heard was shrapnel going ping, ping, ping.*
>
> *—Guzda*

> *Kesnick thought it would be the last day of his life. "Hey, Ted," he called. "How do you pray?" I said, "Pray? Willie, just keep that bucket on your head."*
>
> *—Guzda*

> *All it took was one bullet. To this day, I don't know how we got missed.*
>
> *—Guzda*[75]

---

[75] Ibid.

At the Battle of Normandy, they were on *PC 552*, back-to-back, shooting at the enemy with their 20 mms. Each served one of the aft guns. Neither suffered a scratch.

> *The resistance to the landing was heavy. The beach was not secured till 2:30 in the afternoon…we lost over 3,000…then finally our planes did the job. I couldn't count the number (of) planes that went over. We couldn't sleep. All hell had broken loose.*
>
> —*Guzda*[76]

Roland "Nick" Stine

Nick Stine Jr. was part of one of the last American generations to plow its fields behind a mule. He joined the navy before Pearl Harbor, leaving high school before he graduated to do so. To his last days, he liked to refer to himself as a "coon ass" from Louisiana, to the consternation of his family.

He was officially a radioman aboard the USS *PC 552* and was present at the Battle of Normandy. As patrol craft

Figure 71. Pat and Nick Stine
This is the wedding picture of Patricia Waldrop and Nick Stine, married 12 June 1946, two years to the month after Nick's service at D-Day. Source: Stacy Stine Cary (daughter).

were informal, he also worked on sonar and served a gun. He found listening for submarines while sitting on the top of the ship to be very peaceful. He was also proud of his eyesight, and he always thought that was the reason he was allowed to serve a gun. He made

---

[76] Ibid.

money cutting sailors' hair and pressing their clothes. That became irrelevant on D-Day.

Nick related his experiences in an interview published by *The Montgomery County Courier* on 06 June 2015, seventy-one years after D-Day:

> *"We were faced… with trying to support the landing," Stine said. "I had, invariably, a lot of fire. In our case, we were on the bridge, so it was a lot of 20mm[77] stuff. (The gun isn't) a big one, but that's what it took to protect the troops that were landing.*

> *"There were soldiers there struggling to make the beach and they couldn't do it," he said. "We either went over, or had someone go over, to save them. That's the way the damn war was. It was a lot of experience and God bless me."[78]*

Figure 72. Sam Raup
On his mother's back porch in New Jersey. Source: David Raup (son).

He particularly remembered seeing a German warship and unloading the 20 mm in the German warship's direction. The warship did not think that was funny and came back and opened up on him. The return fire cut all

---

[77] Note: An infantryman would never consider 20 mm small. It is all in perspective.

[78] Steven Green, "Montgomery County veteran remembers Battle of Normandy," *The Montgomery County Courier*, 06 June 2015.

the halyards (rigging lines) on the flag bridge, and they all came down on him.

It wasn't much to remember, but it won't go away either.[79]

Sam Raup

Sam Raup quit school to join the navy and was sent to Finger Lakes, New York, for training. He was rushed from boot camp due to the urgent need for sailors. In a hurry, he had a last meal in the mess hall before embarking on a train for New York with the rest of his graduating class, hanging his pea jacket on a hook, like everyone else did. When he went to retrieve his pea jacket from the hook, it was gone. He assumed someone had taken his by accident—they're all identical—so he took another. It turned out there was a criminal ring stealing pea jackets. As Sam was found wearing a pea jacket not his, he was assumed to be part of the ring and thrown in the brig. The confusion was soon cleared up, but he'd missed his train, and his graduating class was assigned without him. Accordingly, he arrived later by himself and was assigned to the *PC 552*. Where his classmates wound up being assigned and what happened to them, he never knew. It could be that the mishap with the pea jacket saved his life. He didn't feel robbed—he found D-Day to be more than sufficient for one lifetime.

With his son by his side, Sam Raup recounted those times in an interview published by *Penn State Live* entitled "Harrisburg-area veteran Sam Raup recalls D-Day duties on patrol craft off Normandy coast":

---

[79] Ibid.

The Germans were on the beach shooting at the ships and we had to shoot back at them. A lot of guys died that day.

—Sam Raup

He said there were bullet holes all around him, and he was amazed he didn't get hit.

—David Raup (son)

"We were tough," Sam said, adding they didn't think about their close calls much. "We were just grateful to be alive."

—Sam Raup[80]

Sam Raup's son, David, also recounted stories he had heard from his father:

Samuel E. Raup Jr. said that he was the youngest sailor on PC-552, born on 10/23/25. On D-Day, he was 18 years 9 months old…One day he witnessed something brutal that troubled him for the rest of his years.

He said that he saw a line of German prisoners being marched onto the beach. They were guarded by two men with guns, one man on each end of the line of prisoners. The prisoners were required to march with their hands behind their heads while they walked.

After they got down onto the beach, he reported that a third man used a gun to shoot all the prisoners while they stood there with their hands behind their heads. Each prisoner fell and remained on the ground until

---

[80] Barbara Miller, "Harrisburg-area veteran Sam Raup recalls D-Day duties on patrol craft off Normandy coast," *Penn State Live*. Accessed 21 February 2015.

they died. And not all of them died immediately. He recalled hearing men calling, "Vassa! Vassa!" [sic]. This word is spelled the way it was pronounced. The way Sam pronounced it. I believe the actual German word for water is wasser. Though I don't speak German.

After the prisoners were shot, the men marching the prisoners from each end of the line seemed to shrug and turned around and walked away. This was later confirmed to be the order of the day as the assault forces were not sure they would be successful and could not afford to risk keeping prisoners."

Note: Prior to D-Day, a rumor circulated among the American soldiers that they were to shoot all prisoners. The name of the general who supposedly issued that order changed from version to version. No evidence has been found that such an order was issued, but many American soldiers believed the rumor.[81]

A. Bradley Moll

Lt. A. (Albert) Bradley Moll was the XO of the USS *PC 552* during the Battle of Normandy and later its CO. He and his twin brother, Lt.

Figure 73. The Moll brothers
Lt. Graydon Moll on the left and Lt. Bradley Moll on the right.
Source: Brodie Moll, Lt. Bradley Moll's nephew and Lt. Graydon Moll's son.

H. (Henry) Graydon Moll, hailed from Dixon, Illinois—also the hometown of Ronald Reagan. The Moll brothers and Reagan knew

---

[81] Stephen E. Ambrose, *Citizen Soldiers* (New York: Simon & Schuster, 1997).

one another well, and Reagan liked to tell a humorous story about a mishap Lt. Bradley Moll had while dropping a depth charge. Both brothers earned degrees in English from the University of Illinois, and it showed in their writings. The Moll brothers were well known and well liked about Dixon, and big things were expected of them. While Lt. Bradley Moll was fighting the Nazis in Europe, Lt. Graydon Moll was fighting the Japanese in the South Pacific as a naval officer of the 27th Bombardment Squadron.

Bradley's letters home were often published in the *Dixon Evening Telegraph* and were regarded as literary works. As he recounted in some letters home:

> *It was quite a sight to see the task force gathering in the blue-gray channel mist, grouping from various ports, and destined to control one of the beaches on D-Day...*

> *The sea was a bit roughish for the first tank wave; it pounded as it got up to us. In the meantime Jerry started banging away and I could see the orange balls of flame from the guns on shore. Being first in, naturally some stuff came our way. First two short, then one right over us. Figured he had us but a destroyer had seen enough to locate and let him have salvo after salvo. Everybody and his brother was firing—cruisers, battleships, destroyers, gunboats, planes—what a holocaust! In the meantime, we had drowning men all around us so were maneuvering to avoid the fire and pick up those poor devils.*

> *Our beach was the toughest, of all. Mortars were bursting all over the boys. Finally got our boys on the beach and things improved. The Germans had tunnels all over the place and our boys ran them from one*

end to the other with flame throwers. Snipers went up like celluloid combs.
Saw one destroyer knock a German tank end over end...[82]

The line "First two short, then one right over us. Figured he had us..." refers to being bracketed by the feared German 88 artillery. It was likely the next artillery round would have destroyed the *PC 552* if the destroyer had not intervened.

After D-Day, there was no respite for the *PC 552*.

---

[82] "Invasion of France Described in Words from Bradley Moll: Dixon Lieutenant Was Among First to Land on Blazing Beach," *Dixon Evening Telegraph*, 19 August 1944.

12

Deployments after D-Day

After June 1944

Even after D-Day, the war in Europe was not yet over.

In the wider world

While most of the Axis were occupied by the Normandy landings, the Allies landed in southern France with the US 3rd Infantry Division (the Rock of the Marne), the US 36th Infantry Division (Arrowhead, also colloquially referred to as the Texas Army), and the US 45th Infantry Division (Thunderbird), followed up with the French Army B. The Axis were forced to withdraw. During the rest of 1944, the Allies made their way through France, entering Germany in December. At that time, the Battle of the Bulge, the Germans' last-ditch effort, began. In the Pacific, the United States won the Battle of the Philippine Sea in a victory so lopsided it was named the "Marianas Turkey Shoot." Next, the United States won the naval Battle of Leyte Gulf, effectively eliminating the Japanese navy. US *B-29* bombers began their massive bombings against mainland Japan. Glenn Miller, the most famous big-band leader of the time and a major in the US Army Air Force, was lost over the English Channel in December 1944.

A German prisoner of war marching to the American rear realized the Germans were going to lose when he saw a huge transport plane from America land, filled with nothing but apple pies. The Germans could not get enough basic ammunition and supplies from their factories a few hundred kilometers from the rear, yet the Americans could afford to fly in planeloads of apple pies from thousands of miles away across the Atlantic.[83]

The ship was primarily concerned with patrolling for enemy U-boats, shuttling people, and guiding arriving convoys into Cherbourg.

Deployments

> *"Cherry," as the PC 552 was then known on the radio circuits, soon began to show signs of being 'tired' and occasional repair periods in Le Havre provided the necessary renewal of life to the engines and hull. (Ship's History)*

The Channel Islands

The Channel Islands are off the coast of Cherbourg and have been in English hands for centuries. They are officially independent but part of the British Empire. The Germans occupied and fortified them during World War II. The Allies decided they were of no strategic value and so bypassed them. Unfortunately, they became a center for E-boat strikes and so were patrolled by patrol craft to neutralize the E-boats.

The Allies instituted patrols between the Island of Alderney and the Cherbourg and Brittany peninsulas. The tidal currents were very fast, and the weather was extreme. The tides were up to forty feet high, and the seas were wild. The gales blew up the Channel from the Atlantic with violent force, and this area became known as the "Miseries" to the patrol craft crews. The patrols exhausted the crews and wore down the ships.[84] Men on the flying bridge huddled in vain from the cold, driving rains behind the canvas shelter.

---

[83] Stephen E. Ambrose, *Citizen Soldiers* (New York: Simon & Schuster, 1997).

[84] Douglas L. Roberts, *Patrol Craft Squadron One, D-Day and Beyond* (Newcastle, ME:

The area was heavily mined. With the extreme tides, the mines would often bob up to the surface, where they could be destroyed by gunfire. Later, as the Allies lay siege to Brest in Brittany, *PC 1233* was dismayed to discover the hard way the Germans had placed radar-guided 200 mm naval rifles on Alderney. They were remarkably accurate, and the Allies had to avoid that area. The *PC 1233* escaped without harm, although scared.[85]

Members of the crew of the *PC 617* actually suffered nervous breakdowns while patrolling the Miseries, and there is no telling how many crew members of other ships suffered the same fate. It is not something one wishes to brag about. The ship spent months alone battling frightening towering waves during pitch-black nights. Over and over again, the ship plunged into the freezing waves in a way that any rational observer would know was for the last time, only to break through the surface again, awash in foamy spray, and continue on its way. Each daybreak, the ship entered a harbor where it could observe shipping, and the harbor was lined with rocky cliffs that were nerve-racking to navigate. Short of food, short of fresh water, short of sleep, the exhausted crew lived in fear and squalor. Some finally broke. One day, the helmsman was found crying at the helm for no reason. Many crew members became unmanageable, and some actually became incoherent. The skipper finally radioed an emergency, and the ship was ordered back to Dartmouth. The skipper, an officer, and ten sailors were ordered relieved by an

> The patrol craft just were not designed for long periods away from base. They were constantly scrounging for food and other supplies and water, always water.

1991), 36.

[85] Douglas L. Roberts, *Patrol Craft Squadron One, D-Day and Beyond* (Newcastle, ME: 1991), 34.

emergency team of navy physicians and psychiatrists.[86] For a time, it was customary to refer to World War II as "the good war." *Good* seems like an odd adjective to use to describe any war.

According to the deck log, the *PC 552* spent its time patrolling the Miseries in the fall of 1944 and the spring of 1945.

During July 1944, the *PC 552* found a body floating in the sea and buried it. Periodically, the Germans would sow mines, and the ship would destroy them with gunfire in the morning, a harsh way to greet the morning sun. In August, the *PC 552* found a floating human-torpedo submarine. The pilot had died from exposure, and the submarine was captured and turned over to the British. Also, Lieutenant Moll took command of the *PC 552*.

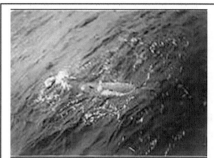

Figure 74. Human torpedo
The USS *PC 552* found a German human-torpedo submarine. Photo includes the dead pilot. Source: William Kesnick.

In September 1944, the British and the Canadians took the French port city of Le Havre, which opened up a new base of operations for the patrol craft, necessitating more deadly anti-mine duties.

HMS *Leopoldville*

In the fall of 1944, the Germans introduced snorkel submarines that could stay underwater for extended periods of time, making it harder to detect them. Previously, the Allied presence was so great in the Channel that if a U-boat surfaced, it died. U-boats needed to surface nightly to charge batteries and get fresh air, so the U-boat activity

---

[86] Douglas L. Roberts, *Rustbucket 7* (Newcastle, ME: Mill Pond Press, 1995), 129.

ceased. The new snorkel technology allowed the Germans to reintroduce submarine warfare, as they could stay underwater indefinitely.[87] Starting Christmas Eve, the HMS *Leopoldville* was sunk outside of Cherbourg Harbor, and the *PC 552* had to look for survivors. In many instances, an important event will be noted in the deck log with a few terse sentences. This is one.

The Allies were desperate to get as many troops and supplies as possible across the English Channel to the European Theater of Operations as quickly as possible. In the process, they cut corners.

The HMS *Leopoldville* sailed from England officered by the Royal Navy, crewed by Belgians, captained by a non-English-speaking Belgian, and crammed with 2,223 American fighting men of the 262nd and 264th Regiments of the 66th Infantry Division (the Black Panthers). The ship was a former luxury liner designed to carry 360 passengers.

Figure 75. 1944 campaign poster
Source: Library of Congress.

Speed was the number-one consideration. No lifeboats were hung over the side, there were inadequate life jackets, and the crew didn't practice any lifeboat or abandon-ship drills.

When the HMS *Leopoldville* took a torpedo, the Royal Navy officers and the Belgian crew took off, leaving the Americans—who had no knowledge of what was going on—to their fate. Eight hundred and

---

[87] Douglas L. Roberts, *Patrol Craft Squadron One, D-Day and Beyond* (Newcastle, ME: 1991), 38.

two Americans died, although no Britons or Belgians died. Most Americans who did not die were hospitalized after making it to Cherbourg, effectively wiping out a complete regiment.

This incident was kept secret for decades in the interest of Allied unity.

> *That Christmas Eve, when I with so many others jumped into the sea filled with oh so many boys crying out to God and Mother is just something I do not wish to recall.*
>
> —Pvt. George Baker[88]

This is what the *PC 552* dealt with on Christmas Eve 1944.

After Christmas

The day after Christmas, the PC *552* sounded General Quarters and rushed to help two British destroyers, HMS *Capel* and HMS *Affleck*. Both had received torpedoes from the German submarine *U-486* off the coast of Cherbourg, France, at about 1400.

The HMS *Capel* and the HMS *Affleck* were good symbols of the British-American alliance during World War II, as they both began as American destroyers built in 1943. The HMS *Capel* was originally to be the USS *Wintle* but was reassigned to the British while under construction. The HMS *Affleck* began life as the USS *Oswald* and was also reassigned to the British. Both of these transfers were made under the Lend-Lease program.

The HMS *Capel* was primarily involved with patrolling the home waters of the United Kingdom, although it did some remote screening on D-Day. The HMS *Affleck* was credited with being involved in the sinking of four U-boats during its short life.

The HMS *Capel* was floating when the *PC 552* arrived, but it sank soon afterward with the loss of her captain, eight other officers, and

---

[88] Stephen E. Ambrose, *Citizen Soldiers* (New York: Simon & Schuster, 1997).

sixty-seven additional men. The HMS *Affleck* was towed back into port, where it was declared a constructive total loss.

I have included a summary of the deck log for 1944 after D-Day in appendix H.

1945

With the Germans, it was not over until it was over.

In the wider world

In January 1945, the Allies landed in the Philippines. The Yalta Conference was held between Britain, the United States, and the Soviets. Germany fell, and Hitler committed suicide. President Roosevelt died. The first German death camps were liberated, and the horrors were exposed. Iwo Jima and Okinawa fell, and among the Japanese, it was a common saying that there were so many American submarines, one could walk from Singapore to Japan by stepping on American submarine periscopes.[89] The Americans had air superiority over Japan and shot up everything that moved on the mainland. The American B-29 bombing runs were intense, and just one such bombing run on Tokyo, Operation Meeting House, resulted in the deaths of between eighty and one hundred thousand people. The Americans planned for the invasion of Japan in October 1945, in which they expected over half a million American casualties and millions of Japanese dead while tens of million more Chinese were killed by the Japanese. Instead, the Allies dropped two atom bombs on Japan to force its surrender. The United Nations was created and centered in New York.

---

[89] Carl Boyd and Akihiko Yoshida, *The Japanese Submarine Force and World War II* (Naval Institute Press, 2002).

Deployments

As far as the *PC 552* is concerned, it is important to remember that the Germans fought to the bitter end, and the crew fully expected to be transferred to the Pacific to fight the Japanese after the fall of Germany. They expected to continue fighting a full-scale war through 1946 and 1947. Few people knew about the atom bomb.

Figure 76. Captain Spielman in later years
Source: US Navy.

Until the fall of Germany, the Germans held the Channel Islands and continued to wreak deadly mischief.

The *PC 552* started the new year on 01 January 1945 by engaging a suspected German submarine. Later that month, command of the *PC 552* transferred from Lieutenant Moll to Lieutenant Spielman.

During the night of 06–07 February, *PC 552* foiled an attempted night raid against the Allies by the garrison commander of the Channel Islands, Admiral Friedrich Hüffmeier. *PC 552* detected an escorting Schnellboot (E-boat), intercepted the E-boat, and opened fire. *PC 552* chased the E-boat for more than twenty miles, firing on it the whole time, before it eventually outran *PC 552*. The only casualty sustained was Coxswain George Sullivan, who received a slight bruise on the left foot when struck by an ejected three-inch, 50 cal. shell case.

Subsequently, Kapitänleutnant Carl-Friedrich Mohr led a successful raid during the night of 08–09 March 1945 (Granville Raid). That time, the Germans severely damaged the patrol craft present, *PC 564*, killing fourteen crew members, capturing another fourteen, and wounding others. The ship had to beach in Brittany.[90]

In April, President Roosevelt died, and the ship flew the US flag at half-mast.

The Germans surrendered 08 May 1945. On 31 May 1945, Task Unit 2.2 was dissolved by Commander, Task Group order 122.2. The European war was over for *PC 552*.

> *The scuttlebutt from below decks carried the ship to every conceivable part of the world where there was still a war. (Ship's History)*

> *Finally the date was set and it was extremely fitting that the group of thirteen subchasers should depart those Channel waters on the first anniversary of the great invasion in which they had a part. On the morning of June 6, 1945, in column with her sister ships, steamed past the beaches which one year before had been the scene of a great struggle, and fired a salute to those who had fallen. (Ship's History)*

Figure 77. *PC 552* salutes Normandy beaches 06 June 1945. USS *PC 552* salutes the Normandy Beaches before starting back home. Note the going-home pennant from the masthead to the rear of the 40 mm gun tub, representing eighteen months overseas. Source: William Kesnick.

The *PC 552* moved from Cherbourg to Le Havre, preparing to go home. On 06 June 1945, the first anniversary of D-Day, the ship left

---

[90] Douglas L. Roberts, *Patrol Craft Squadron One, D-Day and Beyond* (Newcastle, ME: 1991), 36–7.

in formation with USS *Borum* (DE 790); USS *Maloy* (DE 791); and USS PCs *484, 553, 564, 567, 617, 618, 1225, 1232, 1233, 1252, 1262,* and *1263*. At 0949B off Omaha Beach, the ship fired a three-round salute from the three-inch, 50-caliber gun, commemorating the first Allied assault on the Normandy beaches. The ship fired a similar salute at 1103B off Utah Beach. At 1230B, the ship departed for the Azores, then to home.

> *Although the war was still in full force on the other side of the world, the voyage to the US was much like a pleasure cruise, using running lights, being able to smoke on open decks, and even being favored by a calm sea and fair winds. (Ship's History)*

The ship continued to steam home, most often in convoy, but toward the end, it steamed home by itself due to an engine problem. As it moved from time zone to time zone, this was duly noted and logged, and the ship's clock was changed.

On 20 June, the ship was officially transferred to the Pacific Fleet as part of Service Squadron (ServRon) Two, in anticipation of its involvement in the war against Japan.

On 22 June 1945, the ship docked at Pier 1, US Navy Operating Base, in Key West, Florida, at 1230Q, home after 534 days

---

Excerpt from President Truman's Navy Day speech:

"The fleet, on V-J Day (Victory in Japan Day), consisted of 1,200 warships, more than 50,000 supporting and landing craft, and over 40,000 navy planes. By that day, ours was a sea power never before equaled in the history of the world. There were great carrier task forces capable of tracking down and sinking the enemy's fleets, beating down his air power, and pouring destruction on his war-making industries. There were submarines which roamed the seas, invading the enemy's own ports, and destroying his shipping in all the oceans. There were amphibious forces capable of landing soldiers on beaches from Normandy to the Philippines. There were great battleships and cruisers which swept the enemy ships from the seas and bombarded his shore defense almost at will."

and a lifetime of being deployed overseas. The top song for June 1945 was "Sentimental Journey" by Les Brown and His Orchestra.

The ship then convoyed to Charleston, South Carolina, in the company of *PC 553* and *PC 1225*. Upon arrival, the ship immediately began a complete overhaul in anticipation of confronting the Japanese.

To the shipmates' surprise, the atom bombs were dropped on 06 August and 09 August, and Japan announced its surrender on 15 August 1945. Accordingly, in September, the ship was transferred back to the Atlantic force (ACTIVE Lant). The ship and its crew had received a reprieve from being in another war.

> *The Japanese surrender came before the ship was completely ready and PC 552 was then to know the operations of the Navy in peacetime. (Ship's History)*

On 24 October 1945, the ship traveled to Stamford, Connecticut, the hometown of Bill Kesnick and Ted Guzda, and docked at the end of East Meadows Street. It opened to the public on 28 October 1945 for five days as part of the Navy Day celebrations. Over ten thousand visitors walked through the ship. Bill and Ted were very proud.

The ship then sailed to Tompkinsville, New York, where it had been based for so long and near where it had been built, launched, and outfitted. It arrived 30 October 1945. The rest of the year was quiet.

> *And at the end of 1945, USS PC 552 was back again operating in those same waters in which she has 'shaken down' just three years before. (Ship's History)*

Readers can review a detailed summary of the deck log entries for 1945 in appendix I.

Normandy:
A Father's Ship and a Son's Curiosity

1946

It all was winding down.

In the wider world

There is no period after the *S* in Harry S Truman, as he did not have a middle name. He just picked the *S* to conform.

Emperor Hirohito announced on the radio that he was not divine. The entire philosophical basis for the Empire of Japan had been the emperor's divinity as a descendant of the sun god, so this was a public repudiation of the Japanese war position. The rebuilding of Japan and Germany began, and the United States tested an atomic bomb on the Bikini atoll, giving its name to a new and daring style of swimwear. Winston Churchill gave his "Iron Curtain" speech (heralding the start of the Cold War), and on 31 December 1946, the US president declared, "Now, therefore, I, Harry S Truman, president of the United States of America, do hereby proclaim the cessation of hostilities of World War II, effective twelve o'clock noon."

Deployments

By now, the writing was on the wall. *PC 552* marked time until the government decided what to do with it. Sailors left the ship as they were honorably discharged; they were not replaced. When the ship made its final voyage, it was undercrewed by a third.

On 30 March 1946, at 1615, the *PC 552* cast off for its final voyage as a commissioned navy ship. It arrived in Charleston, South Carolina, on 02 April 1946.

On 08 April 1946, Lt. (jg) Robert E. Gleason relieved Lieut. James S. Spielman as the last commanding officer of the *PC 552*. A decommissioning party came aboard 18 April 1946 and placed the ship out of commission. It was towed to the upper end of the anchorage in the Wando River and moored alongside USS *PC 1214*, and the crew disembarked for the final time.

I have provided a detailed summary of the deck log entries for 1946 in appendix J.

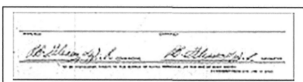

Figure 78. Decommissioning signature
Final signature decommissioning ship from Lt. (jg) R. E. Gleason, commanding officer. Source: NARA.

13

It Is Finally Over

The guns grew silent at last. The people of the United States found themselves architects of the new world order, a job they never asked for and didn't want. By and large, they did an excellent job. Americans felt that World II was a result of the unfinished business of World War I, and World War I was a function of the great powers squabbling over world domination through colonies. Accordingly, the United States pressured for

Figure 79. Logo for the Marshall Plan
A $13.3 billion (in 1950s dollars) plan to rebuild Europe. Source: NARA.

the dismantlement of colonial empires and the expansion of trade. The belief was that countries interconnected by trade, making money and expanding jobs, would consider war to be unprofitable and would be unwilling to upset the applecart. The United States supported international commerce through the Bretton Woods agreement, in which the United States, now owner of over two-thirds of the world's gold supply, made its currency exchangeable at will for gold at the rate of thirty-five dollars an ounce. The other world's currencies were pegged to the dollar, and the World Bank and International Monetary Fund monitored it all. The United Nations was established in New York, the location selected to make clear which nation was the most powerful. The United States also financed and supervised the rebuilding of its former enemies, something unheard of before.

At the time, the people of the United States were told that the mistake the United States had made in the last war was to go home right after it. This time, they stayed in Germany and Japan, defending the two as bulwarks against the Soviet Union and later China and rebuilding them. The United States guaranteed the world economy and safety. Looking back, they were remarkably successful. Although at times it doesn't feel like it, the world has enjoyed the greatest peacetime in its history after World War II.

At home, the United States made sure to not

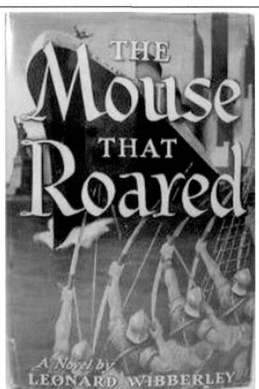

Figure 80. *The Mouse That Roared*
In this famous parody published in 1955, the fictional Duchy of East Fenwick invades the United States with its three men-at-arms and its twenty bowmen. The goal was to deliberately lose to the United States so that the duchy would be showered with wealth, as were the United States' other defeated enemies. Its plans were shattered when the duchy won by a fluke.

repeat the mistake made after World War I with the economy. (The reduction in war expenditures and the returning soldiers created a depression after World War I.) This was one of the reasons for the GI Bill. A remarkable prosperity came about. As the economic, technological, and cultural center of the world, the United States led a burst of worldwide achievement. Something good came out of it all.

New "wisdom"

One new mantra taken to heart by the American people was that they felt Hitler should have been stopped earlier when

Figure 81. *Let There be Light*
1946 film directed by John Huston and known in the US Army as *PMF 5019* claimed that "Twenty percent of our army casualties suffered psychoneurotic symptoms: a sense of impending disaster, hopelessness, fear, and isolation." Film was suppressed by the army.
Source: NARA

he was much weaker. They felt the early attempts to avoid war with Germany were counterproductive appeasements, and this view colored foreign policy. The new wisdom was that attempts to avoid war were appeasement, and the best route was to act, an interventionalist view. It changed how the United States approached the world.

The United States also kept a huge peacetime military and draft, something new in its history.

The greatest generation

Much has been written of that World War II generation, much of it empty paeans to the people who participated in the war from people who cannot understand. Like every generation, that generation faced the problems of the day and solved them. For each generation, "sufficient unto the day is the evil thereof" (Matt 6:34, KJV). Certainly, their times were nothing like the American Civil War. Our family has handed down firsthand American Civil War accounts of tens of thousands of dead and dying men lying on the ground, shrieking their lives away as far as the eye could see, and the need to bury the family silver (the only form of recognized currency, which was needed to buy basic foodstuff) to hide it from marauding armies.

> *I want to tell you all that the reason for my success as a Sergeant is due primarily to my previous training in the Cornbelt Loan and Trust Company. The knowledge I acquired in the good ol' bank I applied to my problems in the infantry. For instance, one day in Okinawa, a Major comes up to me and he says, "Stephenson, you see that hill?" "Yes sir, I see it." "All right," he said. "You and your platoon will attack said hill and take it." So I said to the Major, "but that operation involves considerable risk. We haven't sufficient collateral." "I am aware of that," said the Major, "but the fact remains that there's the hill and you are the guys who are going to take it." So I said to him, "I'm sorry Major, no collateral, no hill." So we didn't take the hill and we lost the war. I think that little story has considerable significance, but I've forgotten what it is.*

A drunk Sgt. Al Stevenson, now a banker, reflects on the irony of the issues he faced during the war compared to those of a postwar banker.

The Best Years of Our Lives, directed by William Wyler and issued in 1946, won eight Academy awards. It was based on MacKinlay Kantor's novel *Glory for Me*.

Nevertheless, the times took their toll. After the American Civil War, it was called "soldiers' heart"; after World War I, it was "shell shock"; and after World War II, it was "battle fatigue." We ignored it after Korea and claimed it was the Vietnam veterans' own fault, but now we call it "PTSD." It is the same thing. The men rarely talked about the war in those days, but there were silent reminders of it everywhere. After the war, many men sported military-style crew cuts, and only after looking back as an adult do I understand they sure drank an awful lot. Pop culture during the 1960s referred to the business "three-martini lunch," and the divorce rate soared. Instead of helping these veterans with their social issues, pop psychology told them and their families they deserved to be happy, whatever that meant. Ten years before, they would have thought happiness was eating regularly and not having to chop cotton for a living. We are still living with the effects today.

The fighting men returning from the war were told they were citizen soldiers, and as such, they were to come back home as if nothing had changed. They were very well treated with the nation's thanks and an amazing GI bill compared to succeeding generations. However, the damage was there under the surface. Many knew something was wrong, even as they pretended there wasn't. We see it in the culture of the time when the protagonist in *The Man in the Grey Flannel Suit*,[91] a then famous book, constantly compares the urgency of his combat experience in Europe through flashbacks with the banality of dealing with corporate political life. Corporate politics were urgent to him now because he was looking out for his wife and children, but they shouldn't have been.

A then famous movie, *The Best Years of Their Lives*, had uncomprehending family members telling returning combat veterans

---

[91] A bestselling novel written by Sloan Wilson and published in 1955, it was released as a movie in 1956, directed by Nunnally Johnson, and starred Gregory Peck. It was labeled a symbol of pointless, soulless businessmen in the 1960s by people who apparently never read the book. (By the way, Peck was a great actor but an unconvincing combat infantry captain. He was too clean and smooth. Infantry is a filthy job—in all meanings of the word.)

to "just get over it" and complaining about how hard *they* had it while the veterans were away to war. This literature quietly spoke to a generation of men.

Wives, girlfriends, and mothers were cautioned in periodicals such as *Redbook*, *Ladies Home Journal*, and *Cosmopolitan* that the homecoming might not be as wonderful as anticipated.[92] Advice was given on what to do if one's husband kept waking up screaming in the night. *Life Magazine* published a disturbing story by John Hersey entitled "Joe is Home Now," which warned, "If your man has been away, he may be a different person now."[93]

A must-see is the film *Let There Be Light*, completed in 1946 by director and veteran John Huston but suppressed by the army, which felt the film would discourage recruitment. The

Figure 82. Bloody Omaha in 1947
A woman on Omaha Beach looks out at ruined ships used in the D-Day storming of Normandy, France. Photograph by David Seymour, 1947.
Source: Pinterest

---

[92] Thomas Childers, *Soldier From the War Returning* (New York: Houghton Mifflin Harcourt, 2009), 93.

[93] John Hersey, "Joe is Home Now," *Life Magazine*, 03 July 1944.

movie shows the mental effects of the war and attempts at treatment and opens with the statement that about 20 percent of America's army casualties came back with a psychotic trauma.

Even with undiagnosed situations, effects linger. Imagine walking in a modern American city and, in a blink of an eye, having all of your senses screaming that you are back, even as your mind tells you that can't be true. The sights are the same, the feelings are the same, and even the smells are the same, but that last is a clue. We now know that flashbacks aren't that unusual and are fairly harmless. The most common trigger is a familiar smell. And yet they seem so real! In the past, the men didn't dare mention these episodes because they didn't want people to think they were crazy.

Most of us don't know how important drinking water is because we always have it ready at hand. Try going without it for an extended period. Coming back and seeing unlimited, pure, clean, sparkling tap water poured into a crystalline glass is a fascinating miracle, one I will never take for granted.

Almost universally, most returning veterans kept their mouths shut until they were about seventy; then most would never shut up. The stories came out as the veterans approached the ends of their lives.

Every returning veteran quickly understands no one really wants to hear his or her story. The audience either disbelieves the story or is repelled by it and the veteran as well. Most learn not to talk about it, although that risks making the veteran look like that damaged man sitting moodily in the corner and nursing a beer. Most did not consider themselves heroes; didn't want to be heroes; and given the chance, would have declined the honor. None can blame them. Paeans to a great generation are nice, but it may be better, from time to time, to pass a few minutes in quiet sympathy for the hard times

153

these people with feet of clay experienced, as people have experienced in the past, experience now, and will experience in the future.

14
The Fate of the *PC 552*

On 17 May 1946, the ship was deemed "not essential to the defense of the US."[94] On 05 June 1946, the ship was stricken from the navy's registry of ships, and on 06 December 1946, the *PC 522* was sold to the maritime commission, the predecessor to the maritime administration (MARAD) "for disposal." While the navy retained records of the sale, the maritime commission has retained no records of receiving the ship or of disposing of it. It has not been included in a list of ships sold to private citizens nor of those transferred to foreign powers. There is no record of the ship's ultimate fate.

This was not unusual for the times. The speed at which the United States mobilized is matched only by the speed with which it demobilized after the war. Without a war, these ships were not worth the money to maintain them.

There was a huge push to convert the US economy from a war basis to a peacetime basis. People were flush with money because of the booming wartime economy but

Figure 83. The Ruptured Duck
Honorable Service Lapel Button (a.k.a. "The Ruptured Duck"). Military were not allowed to own civilian clothes during wartime. Accordingly, people being mustered out wore their military uniforms for a few months. They were issued these buttons and patches to establish that they had been legitimately discharged and were not AWOL.

---

[94] Navy Vessel History Card. Source: NARA.

could not buy anything, because no consumer goods were available. Neil McBride, who served on the *PC 470*, summed it up well:

> *A short time after I was discharged in December of 1945 I was shopping for a pair of slacks in the largest men's clothing store in Erie, PA. They had six pair. They were all one size (not mine). They were Marine Green in color. There were no other choices.*[95]

People wanted houses and cars and normal lives and children to make it all mean something.[96] Many patrol craft were immediately scrapped, and the steel reentered the peacetime economy. That is probably the fate of the *PC 552*. It probably lives on as Fords and Chevrolets, or perhaps later as BMWs and Acuras.

The last words

Bill Kesnick and Ted Guzda
Bill got out of the navy in 1947, married Vera, and had two children. He opened a liquor store in Stamford, Connecticut. Ted married Helen and had four children. He tried to make a career of the navy but found it too hard on his young family, so he mustered out and became a police officer.

---

[95] W. Neil McBride Sr., *When in All Ways Ready for Sea* (St. Petersburg, FL: Attraction Central Publishing, 2009), 7.

[96] George Atkin, a US soldier in the European Theater of Operations who came home on the *Queen Mary*, was a quiet, unassuming, good man; he never had a bad word for anyone, but the Germans troubled him after the war. In particular, he resented their practice of stringing piano wire across roads in Germany, cutting off the heads of unsuspecting Americans riding in jeeps. We privately spoke over bourbon libations offered to the gods and steaks he grilled to perfection many times. I treasure those memories.

Normandy:
A Father's Ship and a Son's Curiosity

Bill was a Radarman when not at General Quarters. He remembered (during a phone call 18 December 2017) the accident that crumpled the bow of the ship in late May 1944. He watched the whole thing on the radar screen and tried to warn the skipper, but it was too late. The other craft was a LCT (R) full of high explosives. The anxiety the crew felt was a concern the damage to the ship might prevent them from participating in D-Day. Thankfully, the SeaBees repaired the ship in time.

Once, while in the English Channel after D-Day, he made a solid radar contact. Alarms pierced the ocean air and echoed across the ocean surface as the ship sounded General Quarters, and the men all jumped out of their sacks and raced to their battle stations. The *PC 552* readied to send another U-boat to oblivion. Just before the attack was launched, the target broached the surface in a burst of spray right in front of the ship. The ship had to quickly bear starboard to miss it. It was a whale!

He remembered a rough but ready crew, and his best friend after Ted was Larry Sullivan, a fellow plank owner, whom he visited years after the war. He never wanted to revisit the old battle sites in Europe.

Bill is living as of this book's publication and seems like a gentle soul. He has an accent one now rarely finds outside of World War II movies. His knees are severely arthritic, and he is in a lot of pain when he walks. He answers his own telephone and is looked after by his family.

I was just nineteen…

—Kesnick[97]

---

[97] Angela Carella, "'They Have the Same Angel.' Buddies Reflect on Surviving D-Day," *The Stamford Advocate*, 06 June 2005.

Normandy was hell, we didn't expect to come back when we went in...we were under tons of fire night and day, mines, aerial bombs...guns...

—Guzda[98]

When Ted Guzda died July 2015, Bill Kesnick was by his side (of course).

Nick Stine

After he returned home from the war, Nick negotiated with the principal of his high school for a high school diploma in return for an essay on the Battle of Normandy.

Nick and his lifelong wife, Patricia, went on to create a successful wildcat oil company and raise four children. He would not talk about the war much until his later years.

For many, many years, Nick lived in the Houston area. He died 21 November 2017 surrounded by family. A fellow veteran prayed over him after his death. Nick, through his beautiful daughter, my wife, is the inspiration for this book.

There's a better way to die. It's not a good experience...It's crazy anyway. That's what war is, what hell is.

If I left a message, it would be war is not worth it. If you come home, you're lucky.

War was a lousy time and it's not something I wear well.[99]

---

[98] Ibid.

[99] Steven Green, "Montgomery County veteran remembers Battle of Normandy," *The Montgomery County Courier*, 06 June 2015.

Normandy:
A Father's Ship and a Son's Curiosity

Sam Raup

Sam came home and married Doris, with whom he had two daughters and one son. He retired as a director of Amtrak. He and his son subsequently visited Normandy and England, where the ship berthed. He was giddy most of the time during the visit; when asked why, he said he never imagined he would survive to have a son he could take to visit these places someday.

Like many veterans, Sam did not mention the war until his later years. He seemed close to his son. Sam died in 2016.

We were just kids.[100]

—*Sam Raup*

A. Bradley Moll

Lt. Bradley Moll left the USS *PC 552* January 1945 and was home by March 1945, after two years of warfare. He married the very beautiful Winnie Knapp in 1950. His family was never quite sure he fully came back from the war, attributing this to a fall from the ship's bridge at the end of 1944. The action at that time was the sinking of the HMS *Leopoldville* and the attacks on the HMS *Capel* and HMS *Affleck*. Lieutenant Moll was commanding officer at the time. He died of service-related complications from a boating accident in 1964. After three years, Winnie went on to marry Dr. James G. McFetridge.

The two families are still in contact, and Lieutenant Bradley Moll has one nephew I am certain of. As he summarized:

> *Funny thing about this war business. You are so busy and so much is happening and everyone is so tense, you do things you never imagine you*

---

[100] Barbara Miller, "Harrisburg-area veteran Sam Raup recalls D-Day duties on patrol craft off Normandy coast," *Penn State Live.* Accessed 21 February 2015.

could do. Somehow it seems that you are not in it and all this is happening to someone else.[101]

Together

Constant themes echoed across the decades from these men and their families. I include not just the ones now living but also those who left their impressions behind in passing through newspaper articles and family members.

One constant theme is that they did not expect to survive the war, particularly on their way to D-Day. They felt it was just a matter of time before they caught that round, and they expected the war to go on long enough to make that inevitable. Even if they survived the European war, they expected to go fight in the Pacific, and the Japanese were infamous for giving no quarter.

Another is the sheer carnage on D-Day. The beach was strewn with bodies, body parts, and burning equipment, leaving a dark smudge over the setting sun. The waves ran red with blood. Even so, the real mental trauma for the crew of the USS *PC 552* came from watching the men of the 741st Tank Battalion drown before their eyes. The *PC 552* was responsible for lining up the tanks before they hit Omaha Beach, but it was clear they were in trouble before they even reached the ship. Dodging German artillery while racing to save what men they could and watching them die before their eyes marked the crew members deeply. There was not a crew member who did not bring that subject up without prompting. It troubled them still.

Last is the universal wonder they felt that they were still alive at the end of it. All the adventures, the cutting it too close, and the rain of

---

[101] "Invasion of France Described in Words from Bradley Moll: Dixon Lieutenant Was Among First to Land on Blazing Beach," *Dixon Evening Telegraph*, 19 August 1944.

ordinance on D-Day made survival unbelievable, and yet they survived. They had trouble accounting for that. It happened many decades ago in another time, but the wonder was still fresh.

Reflection

I read a contemporary account of a World War II sailor describing the beauty and the wistful feeling coming from watching a seagull fly gracefully in the air against a brilliantly blue sky and scudding white clouds. It hovered effortlessly against the wind, then plunged to the sea for fish. The sailor *felt* the mournful cry of the seagull as much as he heard it.

Who among us has not experienced that same beauty and not felt that same wistfulness? As he did, so do you now, and that is how you know these people once lived as you are living now. They are not much different from you. Imagine being there—many people like you were, and they did great things.

Worldwide, 690 million people served during World War II. There were 72 million deaths,[102] and remember: for every casualty, there were spouses, parents, siblings, and friends. World War II was an event of Homeric proportions, the like of

Figure 84. President Dwight D. Eisenhower
"I hate war as only a soldier who has lived it can, only as one who has seen its brutality, its futility, its stupidity."
Address before the Canadian Club, Ottawa, Canada, 10 January 1946.
Dwight D. Eisenhower, Supreme Allied Commander—Europe and president of United States 1953–1961.

---

[102] Statistic Brain Research Institute. "World War II Statistics." Accessed 28 October 2017. http://www.statisticbrain.com/world-war-ii-statistics/.

which had never been seen before and hopefully will never be seen again. There are seemingly unlimited stories of heroics and sacrifice (and cowardice) in libraries, old magazines, and on the Internet.

The crew and family of the *PC 552* were just a tiny part of that story, but they *were* a part. And now, through memory, you are a part.

An honor

Writing this book has been a spiritual experience. It was gratifying to bring these men back to memory and, in some cases, reintroduce them to their families. Some knew them only in later years, after life had worn them down, but now know them as the young men they once were.

The world sure has changed. Search for "PC" nowadays and you will find references to "personal computer" or "political correctness." For me, the biggest surprise was learning how dangerous the whole world was in those days. We worry today about the dangers of terrorist attacks, but those are nothing compared to the real possibility of your country being overrun while your family is beaten, enslaved, raped, and killed. Watch your precious children at night as they sleep peacefully, then get on your knees and thank whatever creator you believe in. Although there were hiccups—such as the internment of Japanese Americans—the United States did a much better job of protecting the Constitution than it does now.

For some, the military experience is seared in their minds in a way others cannot understand. From that comes brotherhood. More than one infantry soldier has told me he felt that the spirit of every soldier who had ever served in his unit came back to the unit after death to support his comrades. If so, I deployed to the Central American jungles with blue-clad Union soldiers by my side—a comforting thought.

Normandy:
A Father's Ship and a Son's Curiosity

Equally, perhaps somewhere, the crew of the *PC 552* is gathering on the foredeck, feeling the ship heave and sway, smoking cigarettes, fantasizing about women, discussing the latest scuttlebutt, telling jokes, and laughing, favored by a following sea and a fair wind, forever young.

We remember them still. Thank you for reading their story.

Sources

The following are the key sources for information included:

Muster rolls of the crew of the USS *PC 552*

Monthly, each navy ship compiled a muster roll: a list of each sailor who reported aboard; each sailor who was relieved; and activity, such as promotions. A final list of the crew for the month was provided, and this was reconciled back to the previous month. Each muster was compiled by the ship's yeoman (navy for *clerk*), then signed by the executive officer (XO) and the commanding officer (CO).

The muster rolls progressed over time. Initially, they listed only the crew and ignored the officers. Starting July 1943, they included a list of the officers on an "Additional Sheet." Finally, in May 1944, the officers were listed each month as part of the deck log "List of Officers." For some reason, the last month enlistment dates were noted in the muster roll was October 1943, though enlistment locations were listed until December 1944. The information for subsequent crew members was derived from other sources.

Deck logs of the USS *PC 552*

Another important source was the daily "Deck Logs of the USS *PC 552*." That is the formal name of what laymen typically refer to as the "ship's log." They begin upon the commissioning of the ship, 29 July 1942, and end on its decommissioning, 18 April 1946. They were handwritten by various watch officers on a rocking and pitching ship until 01 June 1944, and deciphering them can be quite challenging. As of 01 June 1944 (the month of D-Day), they were typed. For some reason, the month of December 1943 has been lost. These logs provide basic information, such as the ship's location, direction, and speed.

Normandy:
A Father's Ship and a Son's Curiosity

War diary of the USS *PC 552*

The primary source for the deployments was the "War Diary of the *USS PC 552*." On 29 Oct 1943, the US Navy issued order FF1/A12-1/A16-3, Serial 7152, which directed the commanders of all navy ships in combat to write war diaries to preserve for history the experience of the ships and their crews. The war diary for *PC 552* stretches from 21 December 1943 to 30 June 1945. The war diary provides much interesting information regarding the ship's activities, including personal observations.

Special reports

Also written were official "after battle reports," "action reports," and other such reports. All these documents were originally classified as "Secret" but were declassified 31 December 2012. They are now maintained in microfiche form at the National Archives and Records Administration. A copy resides at the Bay County Historical Society Museum (PCSA Collection) in Michigan.

Ship's history

A brief but important source is the "Ship's History." This report is only three pages long, but it is the best source for understanding the emotions of the crew during its ordeal. It covers the period from 29 July 1942 to the "end of 1945." It was most likely written by, or at the direction of, the commander at that time, Lt. James Spielman, and forwarded with a letter dated 23 March 1946.

Observation

It is good to remember that all these documents were written by humans, who used human judgment as to whether to note something. For example, once in Europe, German air raids and picking up dead bodies from the sea became fairly common occurrences. At some point they became too common to report. While the deck log might mention an air raid on one day, the war diary might make no mention of it. A week later, the opposite might be true.

Also true is that quality changed from yeoman to yeoman. It is interesting to see the sea stains, penciled tic marks, coffee stains, and scotch tape repairs on documents clearly created by real people in a real event.

Reports of casualties tended to grow after the official report as more information came in. Casualties may be understated depending on the date of the report used.

Lastly, it is astonishing to me that no one has compiled a single list of such things as which Americans earned which medals. (There are many other examples.) For example, if you wish to find a list of the people who were awarded the Silver Star, a medal that is not trivial, you won't find one. Various private organizations have attempted to generate these lists in good faith, but I haven't found complete ones. A ship is a living embodiment of its crew, and it is a shame I have not been able to find the *PC 552*'s battle star. It must have been awarded one—perhaps two. It would be a shame to think it was just overlooked.

Government record sources

There are a number of places to get applicable government records for this sort of research, but the most important are:

National Archives and Records Administration (NARA)
College Park, Maryland

National Personnel Records Center (NPRC)
St. Louis, Missouri

National History and Heritage Command (NHHC)

Normandy:
A Father's Ship and a Son's Curiosity

Washington, DC

Special thanks to Matthew Moll (no relationship to Lt. Moll) of the NPRC for his eternal patience.

Organizations

Bay County Historical Society Museum (PCSA Collection)
(http://www.bchsmuseum.org/id29.html)

Patrol Craft Sailors Association (a veterans' association)
(www.ww2pcsa.org)

Books and other published sources

"2,000 See Launching of Submarine Chaser." *Brooklyn Eagle* (Brooklyn, NY), February 14, 1942.
Admiralty, S.W.I. (UK) Naval Intelligence Division, N.I.D 08408/43 C.B.04051 (90) *"U 470" "U 533" Interrogation of Survivors* (Property of His Majesty's Government). December 1943.
Ambrose, Stephen E. *Citizen Soldiers*. New York: Simon & Schuster, 1997.
Atkinson, Rick. *An Army at Dawn*. New York: Henry Holt and Company, 2002.
"Rescue 44 Men of Sunken Destroyer." *Boston Post*, November 1, 1941.
Bureau of Naval Personnel, Naval Orientation. *NAVPERS 16138-A*. December 1948.
Carella, Angela. "'They Have the Same Angel.' Buddies Reflect on Surviving D-Day." *The Stamford Advocate* (Stamford, CT), June 6, 2005.
Cherrett, Martin. "The 'Great Gale' wrecks the Mulberry Harbors." *World War II Today*. Accessed September 9, 2017. www.ww2.com.
Childers, Thomas. *Soldier from the War Returning*. New York: Houghton Mifflin Harcourt, 2009.

Cooke, C. M., Jr. *Amphibious Operations Invasion of Northern France Western Task Force.* COMINCH P-006. October 21, 1944.

Department of the Navy, Bureau of Naval Personnel. "Information Bulletin, Number 306." September 1942.

Domenech, Ligia T. *Imprisoned in the Caribbean: The 1942 German U-boats Blockade.* Bloomington, IN: iUniverse, 2014.

Ellis, John. *World War II: A Statistical Survey.* New York: Facts on File, 1993.

General Information Book for PCs 552–555. Source uncertain but governmental. Cover page missing (basically the ships' owner's manual). National Archives and Records Administration (NARA), College Park, MD.

Grundman, Vernon H. "It's Rugged." *Our Navy,* May 1, 1945.

Harper, Jon. "Navy admits error, honors World War II captain's bravery in sinking of U-boat." *The Stars and Stripes,* December 19, 2014.

Hartin, W. F. "I Was There! - A Gale Nearly Wrecked Our Invasion Fleet." *The War Illustrated,* July 21, 1944.

Hersey, John. "Joe is Home Now." *Life Magazine,* July 3, 1944.

Huebner, Andrew J. *The Warrior Image: Soldiers in American Culture from World War II to the Vietnam Era.* Chapel Hill, NC: The University of North Carolina Press, 2008.

Hyde, Gary. "Louis Hyde: Crew Member on PC-1225 During World War II." *World War II Magazine.* Accessed February 23, 2015.

"Invasion of France Described in Words from Bradley Moll-Dixon Lieutenant Was Among First to Land on Blazing Beach." *Dixon Evening Telegraph* (Dixon, IL), August 19, 1944.

Laurence, Charles. "George HW Bush narrowly escaped comrades' fate of being killed and eaten by Japanese captors." *The Telegraph,* February 6, 2017.

Legal Information Institute (LII). *Fishgold v. Sullivan Drydock & Repair Corporation et al.* Cornell University Law School.

Kershaw, Robert J. *D-Day: Piercing the Atlantic Wall.* Annapolis, MD: Naval Institute Press, 1994.

Marine Corps University. "Battle Honors of the Six Marine Divisions in WWII." Official Marine Corps website. Accessed September 6, 2017. www.usmcu.edu/historydivision/battle-honors-six-marine-divisions-wwii.

Matyas, Mark. "173-Foot Steel-Hull Patrol Craft." Patrol Craft Sailor Association.

McBride, W. Neil, Sr. *When In All Ways Ready for the Sea.* St. Petersburg, FL: Attraction Center Publishing, 2009.

Miller, Barbara. "Harrisburg-area veteran Sam Raup recalls D-Day duties on patrol craft off Normandy coast." *Penn State Live.* Accessed February 21, 2015.

Morgan, James F. *History of USS Riverhead (PC 567).* St. Petersburg, FL: privately printed, 1992.

Murphy, Brian John. "Sharks in American Waters." *America in WWII,* October 2006.

Naval Commander, Western Task Force. "Coming Events." May 27, 1944.

Nelson, Craig. *Pearl Harbor: From Infamy to Greatness.* New York: Scribner, 2016.

Newsweek Staff. "Exposing the Rape of Nanking." *Newsweek,* November 30, 1997.

Operation Plan No. 2-44 of the Western Task Force, Allied Naval Expeditionary Force. Short Title *"Onwest Two."* April 21, 1944.

Parry, Wynne. "Fragments of D-Day Battle Found in Omaha Beach Sand." *Live Science,* June 5, 2012.

Poirier, Michel Thomas. *Results of the German and American Submarine Campaigns of World War II.* Oct 20, 1999.

Priolo, Gary P. "Submarine Chaser Photo Archive." NavSource Online. Accessed February 22, 2015.

Roberts, Douglas L. *Patrol Craft Squadron One, D-Day and Beyond.*

Newcastle, ME: 1991.

Roberts, Douglas L. *Rustbucket 7.* Newcastle, ME: Mill Pond Press, 1995.

Roosevelt, Franklin D. "Fireside Chat number 18," September 11, 1941. Accessed July 4, 2017. www.youtube.com/watch?v=fUWJX-j1xws.

Smith, K. Annabelle. "A WWII Propaganda Campaign Popularized the Myth That Carrots Help You See in the Dark." *The Smithsonian,* August 13, 2013.

Statistic Brain Research Institute. "World War II Statistics." Accessed October 28, 2017. http://www.statisticbrain.com/world-war-ii-statistics/.

Stillwell, Paul, ed. *Assault on Normandy: First Person Accounts From the Sea Services.* 1st ed. Annapolis, MD: Naval Inst., 1994.

The USS Panay Memorial Website. "Suddenly and Deliberately Attacked! The Story of the Panay Incident." Accessed March 25, 2018. http://usspanay.org/attacked.shtml.

Tokyo Nichi Nichi Shimbun, December 13, 1937.

Turnbull, Grant. "In pictures: The wrecks of D-Day, 70 years on." NRI Digital, December 10, 2013. https://www.naval-technology.com/features/featurepicture-the-wrecks-of-d-day-70-years-on-4143459/.

United States Navy Memorial. http://navylog.navymemorial.org.

United States Treasury Department: Bureau of Customs. "Merchant Vessels of the United States 1947." January 1, 1947.

US Navy. "PC 552 Vessel History Card." Source: NARA.

Veigele, William J. *PC Patrol Craft of World War II: a history of the ships and their crews.* Santa Barbara, CA: Astral Publishing, 1998.

White, Chris. "RFA Berta." *Historical RFA.*

Williams, Greg H. *World War II US Navy Vessels in Private Hands.* Jefferson, NC: McFarland & Company Inc., 2013.

Wood, Ursula, "We Can Do It!" *New Moon* 12, no. 1 (2004).

Normandy:
A Father's Ship and a Son's Curiosity

Personal interviews

Kensick, William (Bill) and family.

Stine, Roland (Nick) and family.

Family members of Robert David, Ted Guzda, A. Bradley Moll, Frank E. Pierce, J. Ross Pilling, and Samuel E. Raup.

Appendix A
Crew

Last Name	First Name	Place of Enlistment	Date Reported on Board	Date Transferred	No. of Days
Acton	Raymond Gordon	Louisville, KY	30 Jul 1942	03 Sep 1942	35
Allison	Curtis E.	Philadelphia, PA	28 Aug 1945	19 Sep 1945	22
Anderson	Elmore Roy	Boston, MA	23 Mar 1946	18 Apr 1946	26
Astin	Robert Henry	New York, NY	30 Jul 1942	18 Aug 1942	19
Avripas	Cordus (n)	St. Louis, MO	31 Oct 1942	09 Mar 1943	129
Bailey	Richard Elbert	Providence, RI	25 Jun 1943	17 Apr 1946	1,027
Barrett	Robert (n)	Cincinnati, OH	25 Aug 1943	02 Jan 1944	130
Barty	Lowell Wayne	St. Louis, MO	19 Aug 1942	18 Dec 1943	486
Beach	Dallas Banker	Pittsburg, PA	30 Jul 1942	01 Jun 1943	306
Beasley	Harold Douglas	Lansing, MI	19 Jan 1946	17 Apr 1946	88
Beaule	Leo R.	Lewiston, MA	02 Aug 1945	15 Mar 1946	225
Bell	Marvin P.	Plymouth, MI	02 Aug 1945	18 Apr 1946	259
Bellhouse	Fred C.	Exeter, CA	15 Aug 1945	18 Apr 1946	246
Bergh	Harry Wilhelm	New York, NY	19 Sep 1942	22 Aug 1945	1,068
Berner	Charles George, Jr.	Buffalo, NY	08 Jan 1946	16 Apr 1946	98
Blankenship	Vernon (n)		02 Aug 1945	18 Apr 1946	259
Blatsos	William (n)	Cleveland, OH	02 Aug 1945	02 Mar 1946	212
Brandon	John Walter	Dallas, TX	30 Jul 1942	09 Oct 1942	71
Brendel	Frederick Joseph	Pittsburgh, PA	24 May 1943	16 Feb 1946	999
Breton	Camil Oscar	Manchester, NH	25 Jun 1943	01 Sep 1945	799
Briggs	Robert Nelson	Portland, OR	30 Jul 1942	19 Mar 1943	232
Brogis	John George	Shenandoah, PA	20 Nov 1945	18 Apr 1946	149
Brown	Irwin Martin	St. Louis, MO	30 Jul 1942	11 Mar 1943	224
Brusca	Vincent Joseph	New York, NY	20 Nov 1943	06 Jan 1945	413
Burleson	Elzie (n)	Hamilton, AL	02 Aug 1945	05 Dec 1945	125
Burnett	Clarence W.	Haleyville, AL	02 Aug 1945	16 Apr 1946	257
Byers	Milton Tyler	San Francisco, CA	27 Apr 1943	09 Aug 1945	835
Caldwell	Clarence A.	Spartanburg, SC	06 Sep 1945	02 Feb 1946	149
Calhoun	John S.	Chipley, FL	06 Sep 1945	18 Apr 1946	224
Campbell	Rufus Wilson	Houston, TX	30 Jul 1942	13 Sep 1942	45

Carroll	Joseph James	Norfolk, VA	30 Jul 1942	28 Sep 1943	425
Chambers	Fred R.	Birmingham, AL	02 Aug 1945	18 Apr 1946	259
Charles	Buford America	Bristol City, VA	13 Oct 1945	05 Dec 1945	53
Choate	James W.	Marion, IL	02 Aug 1945	18 Apr 1946	259
Choquette	Emile Paul	Springfield, MA	29 Jan 1943	14 Feb 1945	747
Christensen	Robert Benjamin	Chicago, IL	30 Jul 1942	01 Mar 1943	214
Christofferson	Harland Hyde	Waterbury, CT	06 Jan 1945	09 Aug 1945	215
Christopher	Junior L.	Fort Payne, AL	02 Aug 1945	18 Apr 1946	259
Clark	George W.	Smithland, KY	02 Aug 1945	18 Oct 1945	77
Cocuzza	Benedict Peter	Detroit, MI	27 Apr 1943	25 May 1943	28
Coleman	Warren Dan	Los Angeles, CA	30 Jul 1942	17 Sep 1942	49
Comitz	Joseph J.	Ashley, PA	02 Aug 1945	02 Apr 1946	243
Culp	John Minus	New Orleans, LA	30 Jul 1942	06 Jun 1943	311
Czarencki	Robert (n)	Dubois, PA	31 Oct 1942	06 Jan 1945	798
David	Robert Lincoln	New York, NY	30 Jan 1943	05 Dec 1945	1,040
DeMoss	Lyle Wayne	St. Louis, MO	30 Jul 1942	31 Dec 1943	519
Dolan	John Joseph		14 Jan 1945	02 Feb 1946	384
Dooley	Arthur David	Boston, MA	27 Oct 1943	02 Feb 1946	829
Doran	Floyd Thomas	Great Lakes, IL	01 May 1943	06 Jun 1943	36
Dossey	Thomas Jack	San Diego, CA	30 Jul 1942	31 Aug 1943	397
Dumont	Joseph George	Springfield, MA	03 Nov 1942	30 Sep 1943	331
Dvorak	Herbert Joseph	New York, NY	03 Nov 1942	30 Sep 1943	331
Eyre	Charles R.	Evansville, IN	04 Mar 1946	18 Apr 1946	45
Fifield	Ernest Elwell	Omaha, NE	19 Sep 1942	06 Jan 1943	109
Floersch	John Thomas	San Francisco, CA	30 Jul 1942	24 Apr 1943	268
Frederick	Russell W.	Great Lakes, IL	31 Aug 1945	18 Apr 1946	230
Galleto	Joe Louis	Chicago, IL	30 Jul 1942	17 Sep 1942	49
Gathings	James Clinton	New York, NY	17 Sep 1942	05 Dec 1942	79
Gaugan	Thomas P.	Englewood, NJ	05 May 1945	29 Sep 1945	147
Gearin	Dewey Cornelius	Portland, OR	30 Jul 1942	17 Sep 1942	49
Geweniger	Robert Max, Jr.	Boston, MA	30 Jul 1942	26 Aug 1944	758
Gilbert	Morris Tacy	Little Rock, AR	30 Jul 1942	01 May 1943	275
Gillon	Thomas R.	Providence, RI	19 Oct 1945	17 Jan 1946	90
Glenn	Thomas Earl	New Port, RI	30 Jul 1942	21 Dec 1943	509
Goins	Lloyd Lee	New Orleans, LA	28 Feb 1945	16 Oct 1945	230
Gossman	Frank Henry	Miami, FL	01 May 1943	12 Jan 1945	622
Gunther	Lester C.	New York, NY	13 Feb 1946	16 Apr 1946	62
Guzda	Theodore Michael	New Haven, CT	02 Nov 1942	06 Jan 1945	796

Hajdu	Charles	New York, NY	28 May 1943	04 Aug 1945	799
Hall	Edwin Jack	New Orleans, LA	24 May 1943	24 Jun 1943	31
Hancock	Alton Carlton	Macon, GA	29 Jan 1943	09 Nov 1945	1,015
Hartley	Allan George	Springfield, MA	16 Jan 1946	02 Mar 1946	45
Hayden	George Michael	Baltimore, MD	06 Jan 1945	08 Aug 1945	214
Hereza	John Antone	New York, NY	09 Oct 1942	29 Sep 1943	355
Hicks	Hinson Richard	Green Cove Springs, FL	20 Nov 1945	18 Apr 1946	149
Hill	William Robert	Omaha, NE	04 Jun 1943	24 Jan 1945	600
Hoffman	Harold Harris	New York, NY	27 Feb 1946	18 Apr 1946	50
Hooker	Jack Barth	South Bend IN	06 Jan 1945	05 Dec 1945	333
Hortopan	Lawrence Larry	Washington, DC	30 Jul 1942	31 Oct 1942	93
Hughes	William Nesbert, Jr.	Birmingham, AL	31 Oct 1942	01 Feb 1943	93
Huling	Paul T.		23 Aug 1945	27 Mar 1946	216
Ingberg	Philip Sigurd	Washington, DC	30 Jul 1942	04 Sep 1943	401
Jablonski	Roman R.	Chicago, IL	04 Mar 1946	18 Apr 1946	45
Jackson	Marvin Losche	Indianapolis, IN	30 Jul 1942	06 Jun 1943	311
Jebsen	Frank Gustav.	Des Moines, IA	22 Apr 1943	26 May 1943	34
Jediny	Daniel (n)	Paterson, NJ	06 Jan 1945	14 Aug 1945	220
Johnson	Lemuel G.		08 Aug 1945	04 Jan 1946	149
Johnston	Kieran Patrick	New York, NY	25 Aug 1943	21 Aug 1945	727
Jordon	David L.	Springfield, IL	02 Aug 1945	18 Apr 1946	259
Joyce	Kenneth William	Boston, MA	31 Mar 1944	04 Aug 1945	491
Karpinen	Leslie Alexander	Milwaukee, WI	25 Aug 1943	04 Aug 1945	710
Keberlau	Boyd Elden	Chicago, IL	25 Aug 1943	06 Jan 1945	500
Keenan	Joseph (n)	New York, NY	06 Jan 1945	02 Apr 1946	451
Kelly	Robert Francis	New York, NY	25 Aug 1943	18 Apr 1946	967
Kemper	Sidney Robert, Jr.	New Orleans, LA	30 Jul 1942	19 Aug 1942	20
Kesnick	William (n)	New Haven, CT	30 Jul 1942	06 Jan 1945	891
Kielty	James Harold		06 Jan 1945	25 Sep 1945	262
Knepp	Alvin J.	Joplin, MO	23 Aug 1945	18 Apr 1946	238
Knutson	Clarence LaVerne	Portland, OR	30 Jul 1942	18 Sep 1942	50
LaMay	Louis Henry	Albany, NY	03 Nov 1942	06 Jan 1945	795
Lambert	Francis Joseph	Kansas City, KS	03 Nov 1942	12 Aug 1945	1,013
Lambert	John Overal	Nashville, TN	25 Nov 1942	23 Apr 1943	149
Lambousy	George Gregory	Jennings, LA	16 Jan 1946	11 Mar 1946	54

Lamon	Raymond (n)	Houston, TX	03 Nov 1942	10 Jan 1943	68
Lee	Erskine Kenneth	Raleigh, NC	07 Oct 1942	04 Aug 1945	1,032
Lemme	Edward Raymond	St. Louis, MO	30 Jul 1942	21 Apr 1943	265
Lindsay	Richard (n)		06 Jan 1945	16 Oct 1945	283
Litchfield	William Gilbert	Cleveland, OH	29 Jan 1943	18 Apr 1946	1,175
London	Foster Lee	Boston, MA	07 Oct 1942	06 Jan 1945	822
Lowden	Ralph Earl	Lansdowne, PA	06 Jan 1945	24 Apr 1945	108
Lupisan	Arsenio	San Diego, CA	30 Jul 1942	26 Aug 1943	392
Lysenger	Allen Tilford	Minneapolis, MN	14 Sep 1942	24 Apr 1943	222
Macomber	William Warren	Boston, MA	30 Jul 1942	23 Apr 1943	267
Mahoney	John Andrew, Jr.	Providence, RI	30 June 1943	11 Dec 1945	895
Manco	Lee Otto	Richmond, VA	30 Jul 1942	14 Sep 1942	46
Manfredi	Enrico	New York, NY	07 Oct 1942	22 Aug 1945	1,050
Martin	Alexander (n)	Jacksonville, FL	19 Sep 1942	16 Aug 1943	331
Martin	Damon Fuqua	Macon, GA	30 Jul 1942	03 Sep 1942	35
Mauney	Almon Elmer	Portland, OR	02 Oct 1943	19 Oct 1945	748
Mayer	Frank (n)	St. Louis, MO	23 Aug 1945	02 Mar 1946	191
McKague	Howard T.	St. Louis, MO	23 Aug 1945	01 Apr 1946	221
McKane	Thomas Farrington	New York, NY	02 Jan 1944	15 Jan 1945	379
McKerney	Thomas Rodrick	Kansas City, MO	29 Oct 1945	06 Feb 1946	100
McMullen	Robert Thomas	Detroit, MI	07 Oct 1942	07 Jul 1945	1,004
McWilliams	John Joseph	Upper Derby, PA	16 Jan 1945	17 Apr 1946	456
Meadows	Frank (n)	Richmond, VA	29 Jan 1943	18 Mar 1943	48
Milton	Walter (n)	Canandaigua, NY	06 Jan 1945	02 Oct 1945	269
Minor	Reggie Hampton	Indianapolis, IN	30 Jul 1942	10 Oct 1942	72
Nobles	William J.	Birmingham, AL	12 Oct 1945	16 Apr 1946	186
Palinsky	Rudolph (n)	Pittsburgh, PA	30 Apr 1945	17 Apr 1946	352
Paris	George Richard	Macon, GA	31 Oct 1942	25 May 1943	206
Parker	Harold Anderson	Kansas City, KS	03 Aug 1945	17 Jan 1946	150
Penny	Charles Milton	St. Louis, MO	30 Jul 1942	06 Aug 1945	1,103
Petrikas	Arthur Charles	Boston, MA	28 Jun 1943	06 Nov 1945	862
Pollard	Clayton Crider	Kansas City, MO	30 Jul 1942	28 Feb 1943	213
Potts	Leo Guss	Pearl Harbor, HI	30 Jul 1942	04 Sep 1943	401
Pursch	Charles Dewalt	Harrisburg, PA	05 Jan 1945	18 Apr 1946	468

Radell	Francis John	Utica, NY	06 Jan 1945	13 Jan 1945	7
Raup	Samuel Edgar, Jr.	Harrisburg, PA	28 Jun 1943	12 Jan 1946	929
Reed	Robert B.	Great Lakes, IL	18 Mar 1945	18 Apr 1946	396
Roark	Paul Dee	Elkton, MD	06 Jan 1945	19 Nov 1945	317
Robinson	Raymond Leo	Boston, MA	04 Sep 1942	09 Jul 1945	1,039
Root	Richard William	Manchester, NH	07 Sep 1943	18 Apr 1946	954
Rosebush	James Maurize	Portland, OR	22 Apr 1943	25 May 1943	33
Ross	David (n), Jr.	Nashville, TN	29 Sep 1942	04 Aug 1945	1,040
Ross	Maurice (n)	New York, NY	07 Sep 1943	04 Aug 1945	697
Rounds	Raymond Francis, Jr.	Providence, RI	25 Jun 1943	06 Jan 1945	561
Rubino	Edwin Franklin	New York, NY	07 Sep 1943	04 Aug 1945	697
Russell	Charles Owen	New York, NY	07 Sep 1943	06 Apr 1946	942
Russo	Louis Andrew	New York, NY	07 Sep 1943	06 Jan 1945	487
Santini	Elmo Cyril	Tampa, FL	30 Jul 1942	31 Jan 1943	185
Schillo	Charles E.	Dayton, OH	31 Aug 1945	18 Apr 1946	230
Schmidt	Conrad Herman	Philadelphia, PA	30 Jul 1942	05 Sep 1945	1,133
Scism	Arlee (n)	Raleigh, NC	30 Jul 1942	02 Jan 1944	521
Scott	Charles Paulhill	Macon, GA	30 Jul 1942	09 Oct 1942	71
Segal	Martin (n)	Philadelphia, PA	30 Jul 1942	24 Apr 1943	268
Sheppard	Glen Calvin	Nashville, TN	03 Nov 1942	05 Jan 1945	794
Shestag	Robert Kenneth	Cleveland, OH	30 Jul 1942	30 Nov 1942	123
Shinopoulos	Peter (n)	Boston, MA	11 Jan 1945	11 Aug 1945	212
Short	Adrian Joseph	Cleveland, OH	25 Aug 1944	17 Apr 1946	600
Slavin	Wm Andrew	Lowell, MA	07 Oct 1942	30 Sep 1943	358
Smith	Ray (n)	Denver, CO	30 Jul 1942	31 Aug 1945	1,128
Spanburg	Charles E.	Lansing, MI	06 Feb 1946	18 Apr 1946	71
Speakman	Frederick Samule	Cleveland, OH	30 Jul 1942	02 Feb 1943	187
Speck	Harold	Detroit, MI	09 Jan 1943	23 Apr 1943	104
Spencer	Emory John	Providence, RI	30 Jul 1942	23 Apr 1943	267
Stack	David Francis	Boston, MA	24 Jun 1943	30 Sep 1943	98
Stanton	Jack Richard	St. Louis, MO	06 Jan 1945	10 Aug 1945	216
Steele	William Rody	Pittsburg, PA	30 Jul 1942	04 Aug 1945	1,101
Stefanek	Edward Walter	New York, NY	30 Jul 1942	06 Jan 1945	891
Stine	Roland Nicholas, Jr.	New Orleans, LA	30 Jul 1942	07 Mar 1945	951
Stone	Joseph Leslie	St. Louis, MO	31 Oct 1942	26 Aug 1944	665
Sullivan	George Clinton	New Haven, CT	30 Jul 1942	18 Apr 1946	1,358
Sullivan	Lawrence Ferrel	Kansas City, MO	30 Jul 1942	01 Oct 1945	1,159

Terrell	Russell Vincent	New York, NY	14 Sep 1942	23 Nov 1943	435
Thomas	Gerald Leroy	Omaha, NE	30 Jul 1942	30 Sep 1943	427
Thornton	Talmage Wauren	Richmond VA	30 Jul 1942	23 May 1943	297
Tipton	Richard Lee	St. Petersburg, FL	05 Jan 1945	22 Aug 1945	229
Turcotte	Robert L.	Boston, MA	14 May 1945	28 Oct 1945	167
Ushman	Albert Charles	St. Louis, MO	30 Jul 1942	06 Jan 1943	160
Van Gundy	Earl Paul	Chicago, IL	17 Aug 1942	23 Apr 1943	249
Van Wormer	Richard Dallas	Cleveland, OH	30 Jul 1942	06 Jan 1945	891
Vaughn	Wilbur Samuel, Jr.	New York, NY	30 Jul 1942	28 Aug 1943	394
Vendetti	Patrick (n)	Pittsburgh, PA	28 Apr 1943	03 Aug 1945	828
Vermilyer	George Ray	New York, NY	30 Jul 1942	23 Apr 1943	267
Viceri	Ernest Natale	Portland, OR	02 Jan 1944	04 Aug 1945	580
Viola	Francis Xavier	New York, NY	28 Jun 1943	30 Sep 1943	94
Walker	William Edward	Albany, NY	30 Jun 1943	20 Dec 1943	173
Watts	Richard Albert	Pittsburgh, PA	22 Apr 1943	18 Apr 1946	1,092
Whitten	Robert J.	Rochester, PA	21 Aug 1945	02 Mar 1946	193
Wiatrowski	William (n)	New York, NY	26 Aug 1944	06 Jan 1945	133
Wilcox	Leon (n)	Newark, NJ	21 Aug 1945	18 Apr 1946	240
Wiley	George Gardner	Providence, RI	10 Feb 1945	15 May 1945	94
Willard	Middleton Finis, Jr.	Nashville, TN	18 Dec 1943	09 Aug 1945	600
Williams	Thomas Jefferson	Omaha, NE	30 Jul 1942	16 Jan 1945	901
Wilson	Charles Rogers	Philadelphia, PA	29 Jun 1943	01 July 1945	733
Wolfson	Julius (n)	New York, NY	29 Jun 1943	06 Aug 1945	769
Woolever	Francis John	Albany, NY	28 Jun 1943	09 Aug 1945	773

Note: This schedule is a composite of a number of sources. The primary source is the muster rolls, but from there, they were compared to the deck log and other sources, including the ever-patient Matt Moll of the National Personnel Records Center.

Some sailors may have served temporarily as crew members while being transferred to their new assignments. Though they may have served aboard the ship, they would not be formally listed as crew.

Appendix B
Commanding Officers

Last Name	First Name	Home	Executive Officer	Signature
McVickar	Donald			
Pilling	J. Ross, Jr.	Philadelphia, PA		
Pierce	Frank Ellis, Jr.	Grand Rapids, MI		
Moll	Albert Bradley	Dixon, IL	31 Jul 1943– 30 Sep 1944	
Spielman	James E.	Hagerstown, MD		
Gleason	Robert E.	Houston, TX		

Appendix C
Other Officers

Last Name	First Name	Home	Date Reported/ Date Left	Executive Officer
Mooshian	K.(arnig)		29 Jul 1942 06 Dec 1942	29 Jul 1942– 06 Dec 1942
Covert	Alexander Thomas	Germantown, PA	06 Dec 1942 31 Mar 1943	06 Dec 1942– 31 Mar 1943
Carr	William Lester	Algonac, MI	29 Jul 1942 24 Apr 1943	
Fuller	Theodore	Yonkers, NY	29 July 1942 31 Oct 1943	
Kronenberg	George H.	Spokane, WA	20 Apr 1943 24 Feb 1945	30 Sep 1944– 24 Feb 1945
Finucane	Thomas Francis	Kansas City, MO	04 Oct 1943 18 Apr 1945	24 Feb 1945– 18 Apr 1945
Wiles	Richard	Syracuse, NY	24 Oct 1943 07 July 1944	
Fowler	Glenn Crew	New York, NY	16 July 1944 16 Jan 1945	
Hastings	James E.	Bangor, ME	31 Oct 1944 20 N0v 1945	01 Oct 1945– 20 Nov 1945
Gerton	Bernard H.	San Francisco CA	16 Dec 1944 05 Jan 1946	20 Nov 1945– 05 Jan 1946
Smith	Robert Stewart	Ridgewood, NJ	21 Jan 1945 28 Mar 1946	05 Jan 1946– 28 Mar 1946
Shaw	Walter James	White Plains, NY	18 Apr 1945 01 Oct 1945	18 Apr 1945– 01 Oct 1945
Nash	Robert Stephen	Great Falls, MT	12 Oct 1945 02 Mar 1946	
Glass	Lamar Frederick	Atlanta, GA	02 Nov 1945 15 Feb 1946	
Waldron	Hicks B., Jr.	New London, CT	19 Nov 1945 19 Mar 1946	
Major	Richard Kreider	Evansville, IN	16 Dec 1945 18 Apr 1946	
McCurdy	John G.	Philadelphia, PA	09 Jan 1946 18 Apr 1946	28 Mar 1946– 18 Apr 1946
Fanning	William L., Jr.	Ossining, NY	18 Feb 1946 17 Apr 1946	

Note: Initially, it was not the policy to list officers on the muster roll, which made compiling this schedule remarkably difficult. Additional names were gleaned by reading the deck logs to look for watch officer names not otherwise noted. Other sources, including the National Personnel Records Center, were also used.

Appendix D
1942 Deck Log Summary

Ship is commissioned

29 Jul 1942: "1410 hours: Lt Commander Sassley USN turned vessel over to Lt. Donald McVickar USNR as C.O. Ship was commissioned as USS *PC 552* and colors hoisted. The following were guests abroad during commissioning ceremonies: Captain Paul P. Blackburn USN (Ret), Mrs. J. R. Birmingham, Dr. Paive (?) W. Fuller, Mrs. William Carr, Mrs. E. Kennedy, Mrs. B Campbell, Mrs. V.D. Cutting, Miss A Cutting, Mr. F.C. Fisher, Mr. H.L. McVickar, Mrs. Donald McVickar, Mrs. H. C. Taylor, Miss C. Moss, Mr Feunie, Mr. E.A. Stern."

Jul 1942: Most of crew was boarded.

10 Aug 1942: Photographer taken aboard to photograph crew.

Shakedown cruises and training

12 Aug 1942: First cruise, around New York Harbor. Ammunition loaded.

Aug 1942: Lots of testing guns, compass, engines, and so on. Many minor repairs and adjustments. Minor excursions, at first around Sullivan Dry Dock, which built the ship, then to Tompkinsville, Staten Island to berth, then to New York Harbor, Oyster Bay, and Boston, Massachusetts, to take on more ammunition. The ship finished the month berthed in Boston. These series of cruises were preliminary trials, while the trip to the Boston Navy Yard was for a shakedown cruise, with final equipment installation and adjustment.

07 Sep 1942: To Provincetown, Massachusetts, to test engines, steering, and communication. Returned to Boston the next day. At

the conclusion of this period, the ship was assigned to the Eastern Sea Frontier, which consisted of the coastal waters from Canada to Jacksonville, Florida, extending out for a nominal distance of two hundred miles.

11–15 Sep 1942: To New London, Connecticut, and Cold Springs Harbor for training operations against American submarines. Returned to Tompkinsville 15 September 1942. The ship was then transferred to the Caribbean Sea Frontier, divided into three sectors: Panama, Trinidad, and Puerto Rico.

First encounter with the enemy

20 Sep 1942: First real convoy escort patrol.

21 Sep 1942: Made contact with submarine and attacked. Dirty water observed.

22 Sep 1942: Made contact again. Attacked twice with help of airplane. Oil slick observed. No proof of successful attack.

27 Sep 1942: Arrived at new berth at Guantanamo Bay, Cuba. End of first combat patrol.

Convoy duty

29 Sep 1942: Out to sea again.

07 Oct 1942: Arrived in Tompkinsville to pick up more crew.

Convoy duty

11–18 Oct 1942: Zigzagged with convoy to Guantanamo Bay, Cuba.

20 Oct 1942: To Santiago de Cuba.

21 Oct 1942: Returned to Guantanamo Bay. Made contact with submarine at 0946 and fired upon it. Lost contact at 1010. Arrived at

1942 Deck Log Summary

Guantanamo Bay.

Convoy duty

23 Oct 1942: Underway for Tompkinsville.

29 Oct 1942: Made contact twice but lost it without firing.

30 Oct 1942: Arrived in Tompkinsville.

Convoy duty

04 Nov 1942: Left for Guantanamo Bay, Cuba, in a zigzagging convoy.

Presidential Citation

11 Nov 1942: Arrived at Guantanamo Bay, Cuba. "1629. Quarters for muster. Ship's company inspected by Commanding Officer. Presentation of Silver Star Medal to Robert B. Christensen, Shipfitter, Second Class, and announcement of Presidential Citation." (No more details provided.)

13 Nov 1942: To Santiago, Cuba, and berthed.

14 Nov 1942: Left for and arrived at Guantanamo Bay, Cuba.

Convoy duty

15 Nov 1942: Left with zigzagging convey bound for Tompkinsville.

23 Nov 1942: Made contact with suspected enemy submarine. From 1220 to 1850 (six and one-half hours), a running battle. Two major attacks by ship with help of HMS *Halifax* and airplane. Multiple depth charges dropped by all. No proof of success.

24 Nov 1942: Arrived at Tompkinsville.

New commanding officer

28 Nov 1942: "Lt. J.R. Pilling, Jr. USNR relieved Lt. D McVickar USNR as commanding officer in accordance with Commandant Fifth Naval District's orders NH8/00/J-104365 dated November 17, 1942."

Convoy duty

18 Dec 1942: Cast off to screen patrol in zigzag course. Contact at 1037. Dropped two depth charges. Lost contact.

25 Dec 1942: Arrived and berthed at Guantanamo Bay, Cuba.

Convoy duty

28 Dec 1942: Left Guantanamo Bay screening a zigzagging convoy.

Appendix E
1943 Deck Log Summary

04 Jan 1943: Arrived and berthed at Tompkinsville.

Convoy duty

11 Jan 1943: Left Tompkinsville screening zigzagging convoy.

General quarters sounded and convoy member boarded

17 Jan 1943: 1420. Sounded general quarters. Prepared boarding party. Boarded #33 in convoy at 1527. Boarding party remained on #33.

18 Jan 1943: Retrieved boarding party. Arrived and berthed at Guantanamo Bay, Cuba.

19 Jan 1943: Left Guantanamo Bay on special sea detail. Set special sea detail at 1305 [no explanation of what this means]. Returned to Guantanamo Bay.

Convoy duty

21 Jan 1943: Cast off for sea duty. Zigzagging convoy protection.

Enemy contact

22 Jan 1943: At 0340, picked up good contact of enemy submarine. Dropped several depth charges. Noticed only smell of fish oil afterward.

27 Jan 1943: Arrived at Tompkinsville, Staten Island. Moored. Many sailors released on leave.

Normandy:
A Father's Ship and a Son's Curiosity

Convoy duty

07 Feb 1943: Cast off for sea and made underway to protect zigzagging convoy.

14 Feb 1943: Arrived at Guantanamo Bay.

Convoy duty

17 Feb 1943: Cast off from Guantanamo Bay to accompany zigzagging convoy.

26 Feb 1943: Arrived at Tompkinsville and moored. Significant inspections. Passed all.

Convoy duty

11 Mar 1943: Cast off and made way to sea. Screened zigzagging convoy.

17 Mar 1943: Arrived at Key West, Florida, and moored.

Convoy duty

22 Mar 1943: Cast off and made to sea to screen zigzagging convoy.

28 Mar 1943: Arrived at Tompkinsville, Staten Island, New York.

Convoy duty

02 Apr 1943: Cast off for special sea detail. Zigzagging convoy.

09 Apr 1943: Arrived at Guantanamo Bay, Cuba.

Convoy duty

12 Apr 1943: Cast off for new sea detail. Rendezvoused with American submarine for training.

13 Apr 1943: Returned to Guantanamo Bay, Cuba.

Appendix E
1943 Deck Log Summary

Convoy duty

14 Apr 1943: Cast off to protect new convoy, zigzagging, as always.

Enemy contact

15 Apr 1943: Possible contact with enemy submarine. Depth charges dropped. No evidence of success.

20 Apr 1943: Possible contact with enemy submarine three times outside New York harbor. Contact attacked by ship each time.

20 Apr 1943: Arrived at Tompkinsville.

Important events

30 Apr 1943: Obviously important events:

> "1405: Received aboard from Grimshaw's Confectionary, candy, soap + gum."

> "1503: Received aboard from Maritime Tobacco Co., cigarettes + book matches."

Convoy duty

02 May 1943: Cast off for sea.

09 May 1943: Arrived at Guantanamo Bay, Cuba.

Convoy duty

14 May 1943: Got underway as ordered. Various courses and speeds.

22 May 1943: Arrived at Tompkinsville.

Convoy duty

06 Jun 1943: Cast off for sea detail.

13 Jun 1943: Arrived at Guantanamo Bay, Cuba.

Convoy duty

16 Jun 1943: Cast off for sea detail.

24 Jun 1943: Arrived at Tompkinsville.

Convoy duty

06 Jul 1943: Ship underway for special sea duty.

13 Jul 1943: Ship moored at Guantanamo Bay, Cuba.

Convoy duty

14 Jul 1943: Ship underway.

19 Jul 1943: Moored at Tompkinsville.

Convoy duty

22 Jul 1943: Cast off, underway.

29 Jul 1943: Moored at Guantanamo Bay, Cuba.

Convoy duty

02 Aug 1943: Cast off, underway.

07 Aug 1943: Arrived at Tompkinsville.

09 Aug 1943: Transferred back to Eastern Sea Frontier.

Convoy duty

10 Aug 1943: Underway.

11 Aug 1943: Moored.

Convoy duty

13 Aug 1943: Underway.

15 Aug 1943: Moored.

Appendix E
1943 Deck Log Summary

Convoy duty

17 Aug 1943: Set special sea detail and underway.

23 Aug 1943: Moored at Tompkinsville. Received new guns and plenty of ammunition.

Convoy duty

09 Sep 1943: Underway.

15 Sep 1943: Moored.

Convoy duty

19 Sep 1943: Underway.

28 Sep 1943: Moored.

New commanding officer

02 Oct 1943: "1300: Lieutenant J. Ross Pilling, USNR, in accordance with official letter from BuPers, turned over command of this vessel to Lt. (jg) Frank Pierce in presence of part of this vessel's crew."

Convoy duty

05 Oct 1943: Underway.

11 Oct 1943: Moored at Guantanamo Bay, Cuba.

Convoy duty

16 Oct 1943: Set special sea detail. Underway.

24 Oct 1943: Moored. (Tompkinsville?)

Convoy duty

29 Oct 1943: Castoff, underway.

04 Nov 1943: Moored.

Normandy:
A Father's Ship and a Son's Curiosity

Convoy duty

09 Nov 1943: Cast off all lines and underway.

17 Nov 1943: Moored.

Convoy duty

28 Nov 1943: Cast off, underway.

Note: December 1943 deck log has been lost.

17 Dec 1943: The ship arrived into New York from her last trip from Guantanamo Bay, as she had been selected to go to France.

In Dec 1943, ship was originally assigned to the Eighth Fleet (Mediterranean), then switched to being assigned to the Twelfth Fleet (Europe).

Preparing to cross the Atlantic

21–31 Dec 1943: Left Tompkinsville, Staten Island, New York, in the company of Destroyer Escorts (DE) *181*, *318*, and *225* and the *PCs* *553* and *1225* to escort the convoy New York Section UGS 28 (**U**nited States to **G**ibraltar-**S**low) to Norfolk, Virginia.

25 Dec 1943: Placed in Portsmouth Navy Yard, Maine, dry dock #1 to have bottom scraped and painted, then berthed.

Appendix F
1944 Deck Log Summary Prior to D-Day

The transatlantic crossing to England

05 Jan 1944: Orders came in January for the move to England. *PC 1225*, along with *PC 553*, *552*, and several DEs, escorted a large, slow-moving convoy across the Atlantic as Task Force 69 for the United Kingdom. The convoy was UGS 29 and consisted of fifty-three merchant ships, the army tug *LT* (Large Tug) *221*; the *LSTs* (Landing Ship, Tank) *22*, *8*, and *44*; the *LCIs* (Landing Craft, Infantry) *493–503*; and the carrier USS *Guadalcanal* with escorts. The crossing was very rough.

15 Jan 1944: Broke off main convoy approximately 527 miles southwest of Ponta Delgada, the Azores, as Task Force 69.2. This task force included the *LCIs* (Landing Craft, Infantry) *493–503* escorted by the *PCs 552*, *553*, and *1225* and headed to Horta, Fayel, the Azores. Ship's evaporator broke down and ship was with little fresh water.

17 Jan 1944: Berthed at Horta, Fayel, the Azores, where *PC 552* remained because of intense weather.

22 Jan 1944: Left Horta as part of Task Group 120.2, which included as additional escorts the *PCs 553* and *1225*. Vessels escorted were the *LCIs 493–502*. Bound for the Tamer River, Dartmouth, Devon but was seriously delayed by the weather. There were several false alarms, but the convoy arrived without incident.

27 Jan 1944: Berthed in the Tamer River, Saltash, England.

Normandy:
A Father's Ship and a Son's Curiosity

European duties commence

10 Feb 1944: First European sea duty commenced. Purpose was to test engines and armament.

12 Feb 1944: Returned to Plymouth, England.

Feb 1944: Berthed in the River Dart, as well as Falmouth, Cornwall. Twice, an air raid was sounded, at which the ship sounded General Quarters. The ship was secured from General Quarters both times without incident. The ship escorted traffic around the English coast as well as protected troop during landing exercises, usually in conjunction with *PCs 553* and *1225*.

Death from military exercises

Mar 1944: More routine coastal escorting, military exercises, and some patrols in coastal waters, usually in the company of *PCs 553* and *1225*. Lots of landing and screening exercises. Two soldiers wounded (11 Mar 1944) during exercises and treated by flotilla medical officers: Sgt. Poriotos (hit in left arm by shrapnel) and Private First Class McGirts (hit in back by shrapnel), both of the 16th Infantry. Private McGirts later died. Most of the time, when not active, berthed in Dartmouth, England, near the Oiler HMS *Berta*.

A distant battle

27 Apr 1944: Five Landing Ships, Tanks (LST) were hit right behind *PC 552*'s convoy. About seven hundred sailors and soldiers died.

27–28 Apr 1944: During the late evening and early morning, the ship observed sporadic gunfire and illumination fire.

29 Apr 1944: 0810: "Executed colors at half mast in memory of the Secretary of the Navy and for the dead resulting from the engagement with German of April 27–28."

Appendix F
1944 Deck Log Summary Prior To D-Day

Apr 1944: Yet more coastal escorting, screening, patrolling, and military assault and landing exercises, often with *PC 553* and *PC 1225*. Three air raids were sounded in April while the ship was berthed.

May 1944: Continued prophetic military exercises consisting of assaults, landings, and escort duty.

27 May 1944: Involved with a practice operation, which turned out to be a dress rehearsal for D-Day. While escorting a convoy during a period of zero visibility due to weather, *PC 552* collided with *LCT (R)* (Landing Craft, Tank) *439*. *PC 552* stayed with *LCT 439* all day, then entered port at Dartmouth when instructed to do so. This incident temporarily shattered the men's hopes.

28–31 May 1944: Board of Investigation came to inspect the damage.

01-03 Jun 1944: Ship repaired.

06 Jun 1944: D-Day.

Appendix G
Crew on D-Day

Officers

Last Name	First Name	Home	Date Boarded	Date Left	CO	XO
Pierce	Frank Ellis, Jr.	Grand Rapids, MI	10 March 1943	30 Sep 1944	31 Oct 1943– 30 Sep 1944	
Moll	Albert Bradley	Dixon, IL	09 March 1943	28 Jan 1945	30 Sep 1944– 28 Jan 1945	31 Jul 1943– 30 Sep 1944
Kronenberg	George H.	Spokane, WA	20 Apr 1943	24 Feb 1945		30 Sep 1944– 24 Feb 1945
Finucane	Thomas Francis	Kansas City, MO	04 Oct 1943	18 Apr 1945		24 Feb 1945– 18 Apr 1945
Wiles	Richard	Syracuse, NY	24 Oct 1943	07 July 1944		

Crew

Last Name	First Name	Date Enlisted	Place of Enlistment	Date Reported on Board	Date Trans
Bailey	Richard Elbert	03 Dec 1942	Providence, RI	25 Jun 1943	17 Apr 1946
Bergh	Harry Wilhelm	09 Mar 1942	New York, NY	19 Sep 1942	22 Aug 1945
Brendel	Frederick Joseph	25 Nov 1942	Pittsburgh, PA	24 May 1943	16 Feb 1946
Breton	Camil Oscar	21 Nov 1942	Manchester, NH	25 Jun 1943	01 Sep 1945
Brusca	Vincent Joseph	23 Aug 1943	New York, NY	20 Nov 1943	06 Jan 1945
Byers	Milton Tyler	13 Oct 1942	San Francisco, CA	27 Apr 1943	09 Aug 1945
Choquette	Emile Paul	14 Dec 1941	Springfield, MA	29 Jan 1943	14 Feb 1945

Appendix G
Crew on D-Day

Czarencki	Robert (n)	12 Mar 1942	Dubois, PA	31 Oct 1942	06 Jan 1945
David	Robert Lincoln	14 Aug 1942	New York, NY	30 Jan 1943	05 Dec 1945
Dooley	Arthur David	15 Dec 1942	Boston, MA	27 Oct 1943	02 Feb 1946
Geweniger	Robert Max, Jr.	03 Feb 1942	Boston, MA	30 Jul 1942	26 Aug 1944
Gossman	Frank Henry	10 Aug 1942	Miami, FL	01 May 1943	12 Jan 1945
Guzda	Theodore Michael	09 Jul 1942	New Haven, CT	02 Nov 1942	06 Jan 1945
Hajdu	Charles	11 Dec 1942	New York, NY	28 May 1943	04 Aug 1945
Hancock	Alton Carlton	06 Nov 1940	Macon, GA	29 Jan 1943	09 Nov 1945
Hill	William Robert	27 Feb 1941	Omaha, NE	04 Jun 1943	24 Jan 1945
Johnston	Kieran Patrick	01 Dec 1942	New York, NY	25 Aug 1943	21 Aug 1945
Joyce	Kenneth William	14 Dec 1942	Boston, MA	31 Mar 1944	04 Aug 1945
Karpinen	Leslie Alexander	11 Nov 1942	Milwaukee, WI	25 Aug 1943	04 Aug 1945
Keberlau	Boyd Elden	30 Dec 1942	Chicago, IL	25 Aug 1943	06 Jan 1945
Kelly	Robert Francis	11 Dec 1942	New York, NY	25 Aug 1943	18 Apr 1946
Kesnick	William (n)	23 Feb 1942	New Haven, CT	30 Jul 1942	06 Jan 1945
LaMay	Louis Henry	02 Sep 1942	Albany, NY	03 Nov 1942	06 Jan 1945
Lambert	Francis Joseph	22 Jul 1942	Kansas City, KS	03 Nov 1942	12 Aug 1945
Lee	Erskine Kenneth	05 May 1942	Raleigh, NC	07 Oct 1942	04 Aug 1945
Litchfield	William Gilbert	06 Nov 1940	Cleveland, OH	29 Jan 1943	18 Apr 1946
London	Foster Lee	27 Apr 1942	Boston, MA	07 Oct 1942	06 Jan 1945
Mahoney	John Andrew, Jr.	29 Mar 1943	Providence, RI	30 June 1943	11 Dec 1945
Manfredi	Enrico	07 May 1942	New York, NY	07 Oct 1942	22 Aug 1945
Mauney	Almon Elmer	07 Mar 1942	Portland, OR	02 Oct 1943	19 Oct 1945
McKane	Thomas Farrington	15 Jun 1943	New York, NY	02 Jan 1944	15 Jan 1945
McMullen	Robert Thomas	01 May 1942	Detroit, MI	07 Oct 1942	07 Jul 1945
Penny	Charles Milton	12 May 1942	St. Louis, MO	30 Jul 1942	06 Aug 1945
Petrikas	Arthur Charles	25 Feb 1943	Boston, MA	28 Jun 1943	06 Nov 1945

Normandy:
A Father's Ship and a Son's Curiosity

Raup	Samuel Edgar, Jr.	25 Mar 1943	Harrisburg, PA	28 Jun 1943	12 Jan 1946
Robinson	Raymond Leo	01 Jun 1942	Boston, MA	04 Sep 1942	09 Jul 1945
Root	Richard William	06 Jul 1943	Manchester, NH	07 Sep 1943	18 Apr 1946
Ross	David (n), Jr.	09 Sep 1941	Nashville, TN	29 Sep 1942	04 Aug 1945
Ross	Maurice (n)	29 Jun 1943	New York, NY	07 Sep 1943	04 Aug 1945
Rounds	Raymond Francis, Jr.	24 Nov 1942	Providence, RI	25 Jun 1943	06 Jan 1945
Rubino	Edwin Franklin	01 Jul 1943	New York, NY	07 Sep 1943	04 Aug 1945
Russo	Louis Andrew	02 Jul 1943	New York, NY	07 Sep 1943	06 Jan 1945
Schmidt	Conrad Herman	01 May 1942	Philadelphia, PA	30 Jul 1942	05 Sep 1945
Sheppard	Glen Calvin	07 Jan 1941	Nashville, TN	03 Nov 1942	05 Jan 1945
Smith	Ray (None)	17 Feb 1942	Denver, CO	30 Jul 1942	31 Aug 1945
Steele	William Rody	04 May 1942	Pittsburg, PA	30 Jul 1942	04 Aug 1945
Stefanek	Edward Walter	30 Apr 1942	New York, NY	30 Jul 1942	06 Jan 1945
Stine	Roland Nicholas, Jr.	27 Jun 1941	New Orleans, LA	30 Jul 1942	07 Mar 1945
Stone	Joseph Leslie	29 Oct 1940	St. Louis, MO	31 Oct 1942	26 Aug 1944
Sullivan	George Clinton	05 May 1942	New Haven, CT	30 Jul 1942	18 Apr 1946
Sullivan	Lawrence Ferrel	07 Apr 1939	Kansas City, MO	30 Jul 1942	01 Oct 1945
Van Wormer	Richard Dallas	28 Apr 1942	Cleveland, OH	30 Jul 1942	06 Jan 1945
Vendetti	Patrick (n)	22 Oct 1942	Pittsburgh, PA	28 Apr 1943	03 Aug 1945
Viceri	Ernest Natale	13 Mar 1942	Portland, OR	02 Jan 1944	04 Aug 1945
Watts	Richard Albert	20 Oct, 1942	Pittsburgh, PA	22Apr 1943	18 Apr 1946
Willard	Middleton Finis, Jr.	24 Mar 1942	Nashville, TN	18 Dec 1943	09 Aug 1945
Williams	Thomas Jefferson	11 Apr 1942	Omaha, NE	30 Jul 1942	16 Jan 1945
Wilson	Charles Rogers	27 Jul 1942	Philadelphia, PA	29 Jun 1943	01 July 1945
Wolfson	Julius (n)	03 Nov 1942	New York, NY	29 Jun 1943	06 Aug 1945
Woolever	Francis John	09 Mar 1943	Albany, NY	28 Jun 1943	09 Aug 1945

Source: muster rolls reconciled with "Reports of Changes."

Appendix H
1944 Deck Log Summary after D-Day

07–08 Jun 1944: Ship attacked by, and responded to, enemy aircraft. Ship engaged in routine combat duties, including control of Fox Green Beach.

09 Jun 1944: Continued same duties. Ship engaged enemy aircraft with her full armament at 2339B and experienced near bomb misses close to the stern.

10–19 Jun 1944: Enemy planes again engaged at 0348B on 11 Jun 1944 and at 0342B on 13 Jun 1944. At 1835B on 14 Jun 1944, ship fired upon a DUKW loaded with Teller mines (German antitank mines). DUKW exploded and sank. *PC 552* remained in the vicinity of Fox Green Beach.

19–22 Jun 1944: Lost anchor at 1326B on 19 Jun 1944 and was forced to ride out a gale until the gale was over. The anchor was then replaced from a cannibalized craft.

23–26 Jun 1944: Served as dispatch vessel.

28 Jun 1944: 1432: Recovered body of Thomas M. Stamm, US Navy, and proceeded to Easy White Beach for burial.

28–30 Jun 1944: Routine duties. Received and escorted Convoy CU 49 (Curaçao to the United Kingdom) bringing fuel from Venezuelan refineries.

Relieved from the line

01 Jul 1944: Left the coast of France and moored in Dartmouth, England, at 1755B.

Normandy:
A Father's Ship and a Son's Curiosity

02 Jul 1944: Took on supplies, received two new anchors, and affected emergency repairs.

03 Jul 1944: Sailed from Dartmouth and returned to the fleet.

04 Jul 1944: Routine duties.

05–06 Jul 1944: Each night, enemy aircraft sowed mines. Additional mines were sunk by ship gunfire.

07 Jul 1944: More routine duties.

08 Jul 1944: Found body, secured identification, and buried body at sea due to condition of remains. Information not provided in log.

09–13 Jul 1944: Routine duties.

14–25 Jul 1944: Dry docked 20 Jul 1944. Full inspection. Returned to Dartmouth, went into dry dock for repairs, and left gunnery officer in hospital. Received replacement officer.

26 Jul 1944: Returned to active duty at Cherbourg.

27–31 Jul 1944: Routine work.

01–03 Aug 1944: Routine work.

German human torpedo found

04 Aug 1944: Found German human torpedo with rudder damaged and pilot dead.

05–13 Aug 1944: Routine duty: patrols, picket lines, etc.

14 Aug 1944: Enemy aircraft came and dropped flares. Anticipated bombers did not follow the flares.

Appendix H
1944 Deck Log Summary after D-Day

New commanding officer

25 Aug 1944: 0900: "In accordance with COMPHIBSUKAY 232117B August 1944 and COMPHIBSUKAY 232115B August 1944, Lt. Frank E. PIERCE, 204832, USNR Commanding Officer, was relieved of command of the USSPC552 (sic), by Lt. Albert Bradley MOLL, 130991, USNR, Crew present at quarters." At this ceremony, Commander Pierce received the Bronze Star for his actions during the invasion.

Sep 1944: Routine.

Oct 1944: Routine. Assigned to patrol of Channel Islands. Weather very nasty.

Armistice Day observed

11 Nov 1944: 1100: "Lowered ensign to half mast in observance of Armistice Day."

Nov 1944: Routine patrolling, etc. Located floating mines and sank them with gunfire. Sank derelict ship considered a menace to shipping.

01–23 Dec 1944: Routine.

Germans attack

24–25 Dec 1944: Proceeded seaward at flank speed to look for survivors of the HMS *Leopoldville*, sunk just off Cherbourg Harbor by either a mine or torpedo. Found none, but *PC 1263* found several survivors. Very heavy seas.

26 Dec 1944: Report of a submarine on surface attacking shipping. General Quarters sounded, and ship rushed to scene. Found two damaged ships, both British destroyer escorts, one sinking (HMS *Capel*), towed the floating ship that had been torpedoed back (HMS

462-Affleck), and directed PT boats to pick up survivors. The submarine was nowhere in sight. *PC 552* was now known as "Cherry" on the radio circuit.

27–31 Dec 1944: Routine.

Appendix I
1945 Deck Log Summary

01 Jan 1945: 1225: Made contact with potential enemy submarine and attacked it with the USS *Borum*. No evidence of success.

New commanding officer

Jan 1945: Routine except change of command 28 Jan 1945. Lieutenant James S. Spielman relieved Lieutenant A. Bradley Moll at 1030A.

01–05 Feb 1945: Routine.

The Germans attempt a night raid

06–07 Feb 1945: Foiled an attempted night raid against the Allies. An escorting Schnellboot (E-boat) was detected by *PC 552*. *PC 552* intercepted the E-boat and opened fire. *PC 552* chased the E-boat for more than twenty miles, firing on it the whole time, before it eventually outran *PC 552*. The only casualty sustained was Coxswain George Sullivan, who received a slight bruise on the left foot when struck by an ejected three-inch 50-caliber shell case.

08-28 Feb 1945: Routine.

Mar 1945: Routine. Back to training and some shore liberty.

Apr 1945: Routine, sinking mines and patrolling, except the following on April 14.

PC 552 mourned death of Roosevelt

"14 April 1945: At 1530 B, lowered colors to half-mast in obedience to Secretary Navy dispatch 122351/69, dated 13 April 1945, giving official notice of the death of President Franklin Delano Roosevelt.

Dropped two depth charges on known wreck at 1920 B in position 49°45'40"N 01°44'00"W."

01–30 May 1945: Routine. The German forces on the Channel Islands kept the PCs in the Cherbourg area on constant alert, and this was not relaxed until the Germans surrendered on 08 May 1945.

31 May 1945: TU 122.2.1 dissolved by order of CTG 122.2.

01 Jun–05 Jun 1945: Departed Cherbourg, France, and arrived and moored at Le Havre, France.

The fallen at Omaha and Utah were honored

06 Jun 1945: Left in formation with USS *Borum* (DE 790), USS *Maloy* (DE 791), and USS PCs *484*, *553*, *564*, *567*, *617*, *618*, *1225*, *1232*, *1233*, *1252*, *1262*, and *1263*. At 949B off Omaha Beach fired three-round salute from three-inch/50-caliber, commemorating the first allied assault on the Normandy beaches. Fired a similar salute at 1103B off Utah Beach. At 1230B, departed for the Azores.

Voyage home was resumed

07 Jun 1945: Continued steaming for the Azores in formation.

08 Jun 1945: Continued in formation, turned back clocks to Zone Z time.

09 Jun 1945: Continued on course.

10 Jun 1945: Continued on course. Switched to Zone N time.

11 Jun 1945: Sighted Ribeirinha Light on Fayal Island, Azores. Final berth at Horta, Fayal Island, Azores, at 1630.

12 Jun 1945: Left Horta in same formation en route for the Bermuda Islands.

13-14 Jun 1945: Continued steaming for home in formation.

15 Jun 1945: Continued steaming as before. Switched clocks to Zone P time.

16 Jun 1945: USS *Borum* and USS *Maloy* left convoy bound for New York at 2125B. *PC 552* and remainder continued on in formation for Bermuda.

17 Jun 1945: Sighted Mount Hill Light on St. David's Island, Bermuda. Entered channel and moored for the evening.

18 Jun 1945: Departed at 0800P, but at 0810P port main engine broke down. Returned to Bermuda for repairs. Remainder of convoy left without *PC 552*.

19 Jun 1945: Left en route for Key West, Florida, at 0830P. That evening, turned back clock to Zone Q time.

20 Jun 1945: Continued steaming for home alone. On this day, the ship was assigned to the Pacific Fleet as part of Service Squadron (ServRon) Two.

Entered home waters

21 Jun 1945: At 1210Q made radar contact with Abasco Pt., Bahama Islands. Entered Providence Channel and at 2130Q left Providence Channel and entered Straits of Florida.

22 Jun 1945: At 1126Q, sighted Sand Key lighthouse and at 1145Q entered Key West Ship Channel. Moored at Pier 1, USNOB, Key West, Florida, at 1230.

23 Jun–30 Jun 1945: Began work on ship for assigned industrial availability. Reported to ComServLant by speed letter on arrival for duty as directed.

25 Jun 1945: Unloaded all munitions.

Waiting for Japan

09 Jul 1945: Cast off for Charleston, South Carolina, via Route "Easy" accompanied by *PC 553* and *PC 1225*.

11 Jul 1945: Arrived at and berthed at Charleston, South Carolina. Nothing else done remainder of month. Remained docked. After eighteen months overseas, the ship underwent a complete overhaul in preparation for the war in the Pacific against Japan.

Aug 1945: Remained docked the entire month next to *PC 553*. Japan's surrender was announced 15 Aug 1945 before the ship completed its overhaul.

Sep 1945: Remained docked the entire month. Accidentally was rammed by *PC 553* as ship was being transferred to another berth in same port. Minor damage. This month, now that the war with Japan was over, the ship was transferred to the Atlantic force (ACTIVE Lant)—ACTIVE, in this case, as opposed to reserve duty.

21 Oct 1945: Cast off for Stamford, Connecticut.

24 Oct 1945: Arrived at Stamford, Connecticut. Docked at end of East Meadows Street.

Navy Day celebration

28 Oct 1945: Opened for public inspection 1030–1130 and 1330– 1700.

29 Oct 1945: Open for inspection as part of Navy Day celebration for a period of five days. About ten thousand interested people boarded her during that period.

Back to Tompkinsville and military exercises

30 Oct 1945: Cast off all lines and made way. Arrived at Tompkinsville and moored. Nothing more remainder of October. The ship was back again operating in those same waters in which she had begun just three years before.

07 Nov 1945: Cast off and arrived at New London, Connecticut.

08 Nov 1946: Reported SubLant (Submarine Force Atlantic) for training with submarines returning from the Pacific war.

27 Nov 1945: Cast off for deployment. Ran maneuvers with the USS *Tigrone* and the USS *Finback*. Returned to berth.

28 Nov 1945: Cast off all lines for sea details.

29 Nov 1945: Moored at New London, Connecticut.

30 Nov 1945: Arrived at Electric Boat Co. Victory Yard at Groton, Connecticut.

15 Dec 1945: Various training cruises. Wound up at New London, Connecticut.

Appendix J
1946 (Last) Deck Log Summary

Jan 1946: Training exercise.

Feb 1946: Minor training exercises. Berthed at Newport, Rhode Island.

Mar 1946: Minor test runs.

Final voyage as navy ship

30 Mar 1946: 1615: Cast off for final voyage as commissioned navy ship.

01 Apr 1946; Reported to Com 6 to be decommissioned but not stripped.

02 Apr 1946: Arrived at Charleston, South Carolina.

04 Apr 1946: Unloaded all ammunition.

New commanding officer

08 Apr 1946: 0810: "Lt (jg) Robert E. Gleason, DE USNR 340441 relieved Lieut. James S. Spielman as Commanding Officer of *PC 552*. BuPers dispatch 221640 dated March 1946."

18 Apr 1946:

> 0900: Decommissioning party came aboard under Lt. (jg) Wells, USNR, to make final inspection. Condition of ship found to be satisfactory.

> 1100: Underway to anchorage in Wando River, Charleston, South

Carolina, with two tugs towing ship.

Ship decommissioned

18 Apr 1946:

1650: Arrived at upper end of anchorage in Wando River and moored alongside USS *PC 1214*.

1700: Completed mooring with steel cables and proceeded to let out port and starboard anchor. Anchors put out downstream with thirty fathoms of chain out.

1705: Lt. (jg) R.E. GLEASON, USNR, commanding officer, placed the ship out of commission in accordance with Com 6 letter of 18 Apr 1946: Serial PC/A4-1/NB.

Appendix K
Ship's Complement

Source: *General Information Book. PC 552–555*. US Navy.

Seamen Branch		Artificer's Branch	
Boatswain's mate, first class	1	Electrician's mate, first class	1
Coxswain	1	Electrician's mate, first class	1
Gunner's mate, second class	1	Electrician's mate, third class	1
Gunner's mate, third class	1	Radioman, first class	1
Quartermaster, third class	1	Radioman, second class	1
Quartermaster, first class	1	Radioman, third class	1
Signalman, first class	1	Shipfitter, second class	1
Signalman, second class	1	Radarman, third class	1
Signalman, third class	1	Radarman, second class	1
Seaman, first class	3	Sound operator, second class	1
Seaman, second class	4	Sound operator, third class	2
	16		12

Artificer's Branch, Engine Room Force		Messman Branch	
Chief machinist's mate	1	Officers' cook, first class	1
Machinist mate, first class	3	Mess attendant, second class	1
Machinist mate, second class	4		2
Fireman, first class	6	Officers	
Fireman, second class	6	Commanding officer	1
	20	Wardroom officers	3
			4

Enlisted men—special branch		Recapitulation	
Yeoman, second class	1		
Storekeeper, second class	1	Officers	4
Pharmacist's mate, first class	1	Crew	55
	3		59

Commissary Branch	
Ship's cook, first class	1
Ship's cook, third class	1
	2

Appendix L
Information Still Missing

In spite of exhaustive research, there is still information missing. Regarding the crew, I am missing the information noted "**NEED**."

Crew

Last Name	First Name	Date Enlisted	Place of Enlistment	Date Reported on Board	Date Trans	Serial Number
Blankenship	Vernon (n)	**NEED**	**NEED**	02 Aug 1945	18 Apr 1946	935 87 06
Dolan	John Joseph	**NEED**	**NEED**	14 Jan 1945	02 Feb 1946	808 76 44
Huling	Paul T.	**NEED**	**NEED**	23 Aug 1945	27 Mar 1946	276 28 51
Kielty	James Harold	**NEED**	**NEED**	06 Jan 1945	25 Sep 1945	224 08 16
Lindsay	Richard (n)	**NEED**	**NEED**	06 Jan 1945	16 Oct 1945	224 73 65
DeMoss	Lyle Wayne	17 Dec 1941	St. Louis, MO	30 Jul 1942	**NEED**	668 14 10
Dumont	Joseph George	15 Dec 1941	Springfield, MA	03 Nov 1942	**NEED**	666 03 94
Dvorak	Herbert Joseph	01 Dec 1941	New York, NY	03 Nov 1942	**NEED**	404 06 13
Slavin	Wm Andrew	24 Sep 1940	Lowell, MA	07 Oct 1942	**NEED**	400 91 43
Stack	David Francis	26 Jun 1941	Boston, MA	24 Jun 1943	**NEED**	201 96 22
Sullivan	Lawrence Ferrel	07 Apr 1939	Kansas City, MO	**NEED**	**NEED**	342 11 28
Thomas	Gerald LeRoy	01 Apr 1941	Omaha, NE	**NEED**	**NEED**	316 77 86
Viola	Francis Xavier	28 Dec 1942	New York, NY	28 Jun 1943	**NEED**	710 63 86
Hicks	Hinson Richard	**NEED**	Green Cove Springs, FL	20 Nov 1945	18 Apr 1946	831 21 19
Joyce	Kenneth William	14 Dec 1942	Boston, MA	**NEED**	04 Aug 1945	202 89 68
Wilson	Charles Rogers	27 Jul 1942	Philadelphia, PA	29 Jun 1943	**NEED**	650 85 36

Normandy:
A Father's Ship and a Son's Curiosity

Officers

Last Name	First Name	Home	Date Left	Rank Upon Leaving
McVickar	Donald	**NEED**	28 Nov 1942	**NEED**
Mooshian	K.(arnig)	**NEED**	06 Dec 1942	**NEED**
Covert	Alexander Thomas	Germantown, PA	**NEED**	**NEED**

This information is at the National Personnel Records Center (NPRC) in St. Louis, Missouri; however, I am afraid I have exhausted their patience. If you request this information, please make sure to note this is for nonprofit historical research. You may have to visit NPRC. If you provide the information, I will add it. Please help these sailors be remembered.

Also, I still need any documentation that supports what happened to the ship. It would be nice to see the orders to scrap the ship, if applicable.

The address is USS.PC.552@gmail.com.

About the Author

David Cary grew up in Northern California, including in an old mining town in the Mother Lode country, where he attended a one-room schoolhouse built in 1860. He spent four years as an NCO in the infantry in the 1970s and is an expert rifleman and a graduate of the NCO Academy. He is a CPA and served as the chief financial officer of a company when it went public on the NASDAQ. He now lives in Dallas with his wife, Stacy, and children. History is one of his passions; the other is his wife.